Biblical Principles

FOR FINANCIAL DECISIONS

Biblical Principles

FOR FINANCIAL DECISIONS

By Scott McFeters

XULON PRESS

Xulon Press
2301 Lucien Way #415
Maitland, FL 32751
407.339.4217
www.xulonpress.com

Xulon
PRESS

Unless otherwise indicated, Scripture quotations taken from the King James Version (KJV)–*public domain*.

Paperback ISBN-13: 978-1-6628-2687-0
Hard Cover ISBN-13: 978-1-6628-2688-7
eBook ISBN-13: 978-1-6628-2689-4

Table of Contents

༄

Foreword

⁓

The Bible has principles for every area of life, including money. Some people don't want to hear what the Bible has to say about money. God gave a blueprint for financial success, and it is important for every child of God to understand His principles. His blueprint is **not** the recipe for getting rich. It is the outline for how we are to handle money, whether we are rich or poor.

It is not God's plan that every Christian be wealthy. At times, it may not be His plan for any Christian to be rich. Financial wealth does not ensure happiness, godliness, or a relationship with Him. In many cases, financial wealth, or the pursuit thereof, will distract His children from knowing Him.

If you do not know Jesus Christ as your personal Lord and Savior, that is the most pressing issue in your life right now. You don't need an outline on wealth and money management, you need a relationship with God.

God is righteous and good, and we are evil, nasty sinners. Covetousness is one such sin that keeps us from God. Because we are filthy in His eyes, He cannot tolerate to even look upon us, much less allow us into His paradise called Heaven. But

God chose to spend all the riches of Heaven to purchase back His creation. Jesus, the Son of God was sent to earth to die in your place.

The death of Jesus Christ was sufficient payment for the sins of all mankind, including yours. Though His death was real, it was not the end. Jesus arose from the dead according to the Scriptures, proving He had power over sin and death. He now offers you salvation from your sins as a free gift, if you will place your faith in Him alone:

> *For by grace are ye saved through faith; and that not of yourselves: it is the gift of God: Not of works, lest any man should boast. (Eph. 2:8-9)*

I hope you have found the gift of Jesus Christ. If you have, then enjoy this book as it outlines ***Biblical Principles for Financial Decisions.***

CHAPTER 1

Everything Belongs to God, Not Me

⁓

For every beast of the forest is mine, and the cattle upon a thousand hills. I know all the fowls of the mountains: and the wild beasts of the field are mine. If I were hungry, I would not tell thee: for the world is mine, and the fullness thereof. (Ps. 50:10-12)

We like to think that things belong to us. This is my house. This is my car. This is my retirement portfolio. But nothing truly belongs to us. Everything belongs to God. We are merely stewards of what God has placed into our trust.

A steward is the Bible word for a manager. Abraham had a steward named Eliezer of Damascus, who helped Abraham manage his growing wealth (Gen. 15:2). Joseph had a steward in Egypt who managed his affairs (Gen. 43:19). Elah had a steward in Tirzah named Arza who did not do such a great job (1 Kings 16:9).

Jesus gave several parables about stewards. One of the best known is found in Luke 16, where He described an unjust steward who had been wasting his lord's money. In Luke 12:42, after delivering a parable, Peter asked Jesus if His words were only for the disciples, or for everyone. Here was Jesus' response:

> *And the Lord said, Who then is that faithful and wise steward, whom his lord shall make ruler over his household, to give them their portion of meat in due season? Blessed is that servant, whom his lord when he cometh shall find so doing. Of a truth I say unto you, that he will make him ruler over all that he hath. (Lk. 12:42-44)*

From Luke 12, we realize that Jesus has entrusted every one of us with some of His possessions as a test of our stewardship (management). If we manage well what has been entrusted to us, then there is the promise of more management to come. If we mismanage our stewardship, then there is judgment to come. The reward or judgement is based proportionally upon what has been entrusted into our care.

> *...For unto whomsoever much is given, of him shall be much required: and to whom men have committed much, of him they will ask the more. (Lk. 12:48b)*

When I was a student in college, I worked full time, on top of my studies, to pay my school bill. The first year, I did not like my job. I worked in a warehouse unloading and separating freight. It was hard and physical work, but the worst part of the job was the schedule. I worked from 11pm to 7am. I tried my best to work hard, but there was something depressing about working overnight. I could not handle it very well.

After one year at this job, I quit. I left on good terms; I did not leave my company hanging, but I had had enough overnight work. The school year was over, and I went home for the summer, and found a summer job. I was at the place where I was trying to decide if I would return to college or pursue a different career. Then one day, a former co-worker called me. He had been promoted to be the nighttime manager and wanted to know if I would like to come back to school and work for him.

I did not want to work the overnight shift. It was hard and depressing. But after prayer and seeking counsel, I went back to California to that same job I had left several months earlier. Six weeks later I was promoted to an assistant manager on the swing shift, working 3pm to 11:30pm. I did not know it at the time, but my bosses had watched my work. They saw that I was ethical, hardworking, and obedient to their desires. I was a good steward of my job, so they entrusted me with more.

Four months later I was promoted to a temporary manager, and then a permanent manager, and promoted with several pay increases over the next three years. I discovered that faithfulness in my stewardship led to a greater level of responsibility. And when the company prospered, I received a greater reward than those working under me, because I was responsible for more stewardship.

God works the same way, but on a grander scale. He keeps far better records of how we manage the stewardship He has bestowed upon us. Understanding that God has entrusted us with a stewardship, how ought we to live?

STEWARDSHIP PRINCIPLE #1
The Lord has entrusted me with His resources, therefore I will not use my money in a way that would displease God.

Many devout Christians will speak against gambling, but they have no real biblical reason why it is bad. It is just on a checklist of rules they follow. There needs to be a greater understanding of this stewardship principle because it applies to far more than simply gambling. If everything I have belongs to God, then I need to spend His money in a way with which He would be pleased. Does it please God for me to buy lottery tickets?

This topic will be discussed later, but for now, we need to look at a broader picture. **Everything** I spend is money that belongs to God.

> *The earth is the LORD's, and the fullness thereof; the world, and they that dwell therein. (Ps. 24:1)*

> *But thou shalt remember the LORD thy God: for it is he that giveth thee power to get wealth… (Deut. 8:18)*

Some people spend much money on entertainment that displeases God. Some people spend much money on causes that displease God. Many Christians spend money on investments that displease God. Should I invest God's money into a company that displeases God?

As I write this book, there are several large companies that offer very attractive dividend yields. As of today, Philip Morris (PM) and Altria (MO) are two of the largest tobacco companies in the world and are attractive to many investors for their dividend yield.

Philip Morris (PM) trades below $80 per share and has an annual dividend yield of above 6 percent. Altria (MO) trades around $40 per share and has an annual dividend yield above 8 percent. Both appear to also have upside price potential. Many investors see these two companies as "safe havens" for income-producing investments suitable for retirees. But what would God think if I invested His money into these companies? Just because a company may be legal, does not mean that it is morally right. God desires us to be self-controlled, and not under any addictions, these two companies thrive off of addiction.

> All things are lawful unto me, but all things are not expedient: all things are lawful for me, but I will not be brought under the power of any. (1 Cor. 6:12)

Anheuser-Busch (BUD) is a beer company trading today around $70 per share. They do not have a high-dividend yield, but do have upside growth potential. Molson Coors (TAP) is another beer company trading around $46 per share and has an annual dividend yield about 5 percent. What would God think if I invested His money into these companies? God give a warning to those who produce and distribute alcohol, so would God be pleased if you invested His money into a company whose sole purpose is making others drunk?

> Woe unto him that giveth his neighbor drink, that puttest thy bottle to him, and makest him drunken also... (Hab. 2:15)

What about investing into weapons manufacturers such as Smith and Wesson (SWBI) and Sturm Ruger (RGR). What about the oil stocks such as Exxon Mobile (XOM) or Chevron (CVX). What about Internet search companies that grant easy access to pornography, such as Alphabet (GOOG), or social media sites like Facebook (FB)? What about video streaming services that produce and stream wicked content such as Netflix (NFLX).

This book is not to give you a list of companies to avoid (sin stocks). This is to cause you to ask the question: "Would God be pleased with my stewardship?" You cannot justify a 5 percent yield if God would be dishonored. You cannot justify a 5,000 percent yield if God would be displeased! You must dive into the Scriptures and follow the Holy Spirit's leading to determine if God would be pleased with investing His money into these companies.

There are two men in the Bible who took different approaches to this type of thinking. Moses and Balaam.

> *By faith Moses, when he was come to years, refused to be called the son of Pharaoh's daughter; Choosing rather to suffer affliction with the people of God, than to enjoy the pleasures of sin for a season; Esteeming the reproach of Christ greater riches than the treasures in Egypt: for he had respect unto the recompence of the reward. By faith he forsook Egypt, not fearing the wrath of the king: for he endured, as seeing him who is invisible. (Heb. 11:24-27)*

Moses was not content to live in the wealth and luxury of the Egyptian palace because it was sinful. Egypt had enslaved God's people, and Moses could not stand for that, even if it cost him all his wealth, which it did. As a result of Moses' decision to flee the world, he was privileged to speak with God face to face (Ex. 33:11)! God was His wealth!

Then there is Balaam. He said the right words, but things did not quite go the same for him. He was hired to go to the king of Moab and curse God's people. Listen to what Balaam said:

> *If Balak would give me his house full of silver and gold, I cannot go beyond the commandment of the LORD, to do either good or bad of mine own mind; but what the LORD saith, that will I speak? (Num. 24:13)*

Balaam told the king that he could not change God's word even for a house full of silver and gold! But he still wanted that house full of money. It did not take long before Balaam returned to Balak, king of Moab, with evil counsel. We read about it a few chapters later.

> *And they slew the kings of Midian, beside the rest of them that were slain; namely, Evi, and Rekem, and Zur, and Hur, and Reba, five kings of Midian: **Balaam also the son of Beor** they slew with the sword. (Num. 31:8)*

> *Behold, these caused the children of Israel, **through the counsel of Balaam**, to commit trespass against the LORD in the matter of Peor, and there was a plague among the congregation of the LORD. (Num. 31:16)*

Even though Balaam knew it was wrong, he "partnered up" with the enemies of God and counseled that they send harlots into the Israelite camp to promote fornication among the Israelites.

In doing so, Balaam secured for himself a financial reward from Balak, but he also secured the wrath of God upon himself. What good were his treasures the day he was executed?

As a steward of some of God's riches, I have a responsibility to spend, invest, give, or even lose those resources in a manner that would honor my Lord.

Beyond investing, there are many other spending habits that may need to be addressed. Every year, someone will make a push to boycott certain retail stores or businesses for some reason or another. A few years ago, the LGBT community put out a boycott of Chick-fil-A because, as a company, they take a stand for marriage as the Bible teaches. I would obviously not be a part of such a boycott, because God would agree with Chick-fil-A's position.

However, when a store promotes sin, it may be that God would have you boycott that company. That is between you and God. I have refrained from shopping at businesses I used to frequent due to a public stance by a company. I have to ask the question: Would God be pleased if I supported this company financially? I have determined that, as a steward of God's money, I will not use that money in a way that will displease the Master.

STEWARDSHIP PRINCIPLE #2
The Lord has entrusted me with His resources, therefore, I will use my money in a way that would please God.

The converse of the aforementioned principle #1 is also true. What would please God? Those are the causes I will support, those are companies in which I will invest, and those are the companies I will patronize. There is, however, an understanding that my stewardship is limited. Not every worthy cause is one to which I can contribute.

If God has entrusted me with the stewardship of $10,000, I cannot give, spend, invest, or lose more than what He has given to me. I personally could easily give away $100 million if the Lord entrusted to me that level of resources, but He has not. He has granted to me a limited stewardship. He has also granted to you limited resources. So we must discern what is good, better, and best.

Two years ago, my wife and I were on the hunt, searching for a house to buy. We had our list of wants and desires, and wouldn't you know it, those didn't come in a house within our budget. Upon applying to a bank for a pre-approval for a mortgage (more on that in the following chapters), we were given a congratulations letter saying that we were approved for a $459,000 mortgage.

Depending upon where you live, that may seem very high, or very low. But compared to our income, it was very high! We decided to lower our search to houses of only $300,000, and hoped for less than that (which was hard for our area). We chose to lower our target price because of the principle of good, better, best. A house was a good thing, but what about our giving? What about missions trips to help missionaries? What about having money for food?

I believe wholeheartedly that a $450,000 house in our area, with our income, would not have pleased God. It would be nothing more than covetousness and impatience. One day, the Lord may grant us the ability to live in a home equivalent to that cost, but not yet.

This leads us into one of the most important money management disciplines we can have: a budget!

> *For which of you, intending to build a tower, sitteth not down first, and counteth the cost, whether he have sufficient to finish it? (Lk. 14:28)*

To many, the word "budget" sounds like an evil word. They feel that it ruins their fun. But a budget is just a plan for the stewardship of money. A budget is a proactive approach to your spending, rather than a reactive approach. A budget itemizes your expenses before they are due, organizes your payments upon when they are due, and alleviates tensions and anxiety.

A budget needs to be detailed enough to account for all spending, but can also be flexible, if necessary. Every dollar of income has a name before it arrives, that way you do not wonder what you should pay first.

At the time of this writing, I have forty-two line items in my budget. They are divided into seven categories. My first category is giving (more on why that is first later in the book). Inside of that category I have five line items. A weekly offering to my church, a weekly offering to support missionaries, a weekly offering to support a building program, a monthly offering to my alma mater, and a weekly line item called "other." This "other" line item is so that I can meet needs of others as I see them arrive. Recently, my wife and I purchased new tires for someone in need. We knew we could afford it, because we had an "other" line item for such things. My wife did not look at me and ask, "But Scott, how will we pay the light bill if we buy these tires?" She already knew how the light bill would be paid, because that was a different line item.

On occasion, we may overspend on an area. Then my wife and I need to figure out where the money is coming from. If we want to spend $1,000 on a vacation, but we only have $500 in the line item, then we might need to go to our "Clothing" line item, or our "Christmas" line item, or even our "House Repair" line item to make up the difference. The other option is that we don't take that vacation. The budget allows us to see exactly what we are spending, and it allows us to decide what is good, better, and best.

How do you decide your budget? This is not a simple task. My wife and I review our budget and change it any time something big changes. For example, my wife lost half of her income during the Covid-19 pandemic. So we had to rebalance our budget. When we paid off our car loan balances, we had to rebalance our budget. I was in a car accident and totaled my car; to get a new car we had to rebalance our budget. One day when we have children, we will definitely need to rebalance our budget.

The key to making a budget is to ask the question of good, better, and best as it relates to God and stewardship. How much would God be pleased with my giving line item? How much would God be pleased with my housing payment? How much would God be pleased with my food budget? How much would God be pleased with my entertainment budget? My wife and I have decided that we will not spend any money on monthly video streaming services. Instead, that money will be used for giving to my alma mater to help train Christian young people to serve God. This may not be your budget line item, but it is ours. Our stewardship is limited, and we believe that for our level of stewardship, this was better than a video streaming service.

You must create your own budget with prayer, possibly with fasting, seeking wise counsel, trial and error, and probably a few difficult months to get it right. Remember that the budget is your friend. If done correctly, it will help you determine how God would want you to disperse His money. Remember, it all belongs to Him; you have simply been given charge of His money.

STEWARDSHIP PRINCIPLE #3
The Lord has entrusted me with His resources, therefore, I give away my money to God's causes

> *Having then gifts differing according to the grace that is given to us, whether prophecy, let us prophesy according to the proportion of faith; Or ministry, let us wait on our ministering: or he that teacheth, on teaching; Or he that exhorteth, on exhortation: he that giveth, let him do it with simplicity; he that ruleth, with diligence; he that sheweth mercy, with cheerfulness. (Rom. 12:6-8)*

Giving is a spiritual gift. We are not all equipped with the same level of spiritual giftedness. In Christ's parable of the talents (Matthew 25) three stewards were entrusted with three different levels of wealth to manage. This does not mean we can exclude the spiritual gifts in which we are not strong. Contrarily, we are told concerning the gift of giving that we are to abound in this grace also (2 Cor. 8:7).

Some are more talented in the gift of giving, but we can all grow and abound in this grace if we practice using the gift. We must learn to give according to God's principles.

As a pastor, I am not a political activist. It is my duty to preach righteousness. There have been times when I have given to political campaigns. I believed the candidates I supported were seeking to honor God and restore righteousness in the office for which they were running. Those financial gifts were small. Not because I did not believe in the candidate, but as a steward of God's money, I believed they simply fell into the "good" category, not the "better" or "best."

My primary source of giving goes to God's house, the local church. It is not the only recipient of my giving, but it is the primary. Why? Because it is the "best" category. Of all the wealth God has entrusted to me, where does He want me to deploy that wealth? I believe He wants for me to deploy the largest portion of the wealth He has entrusted to me back to His local church. My local church supports missionaries all around the world who preach the gospel, run orphanages and food programs, start schools, and many other things.

This will not be the same for everyone. As mentioned earlier, if God entrusted to me $100 million to give away, I would not deploy such a large percentage to my local church, because they would have no need for such a large gift. I would seek out other avenues to which to give God's money. But for the majority of those reading this book, your primary giving avenue will likely be to your local church. If you feel you cannot trust your local church with your money, then you need a change of heart, or a change of church.

Outside of my local church, where might I give away God's money? I must, as a good steward, only give to causes with which God would be pleased! If I believe God would have me deploy some of His funds to feed the poor, should I contribute to a Christian organization that feeds the poor and teaches Christ, or a LGBTQ organization that feeds the poor and teaches abominations? If I believe God would have me deploy His funds to provide water to third world communities, should I contribute to a Christian organization that brings water and the Living Water of Jesus Christ, or to a secular humanitarian effort that provides water, but has no message of hope?

The stewardship with which I have been entrusted is limited. I cannot contribute to every cause. So which causes would God hold as highest priority? Those ought to be my priorities also. When determining where to give my money, I ask myself, "Which is good, which is better, and which is best?"

STEWARDSHIP PRINCIPLE #4
The Lord has entrusted me with His resources, therefore, I will also use God's money to supply my needs.

Who goeth a warfare any time at his own charges? Who planteth a vineyard, and eateth not the fruit thereof? Or who feedeth a flock, and eateth not of the milk of the flock? Say I these things as a man? Or saith not the law the same also? For it is written in the law of Moses, Thou shalt not muzzle the mouth of the ox that treadeth out the corn.

Doth God take care for oxen? Or saith he it altogether for
our sakes? For our sakes, no doubt, this is written: That he
that ploweth shall plow in hope; and that he that thresheth
in hope should be partaker of his hope. (1 Cor. 9:7-10)

Every single thing we have ever been given belongs to God, but God has entrusted to us the stewardship of it. And the Bible makes it clear that we are to use His resources to supply our needs. But this must not be done out of order. We must take care of God's purposes first, and then we care for our own!

It was to a giving church in Philippi that the promise was given, "My God shall supply all your need according to his riches in glory by Christ Jesus" (Phil. 4:19). It was a promise from Jesus Himself in Luke 6:38 when He said, "Give and it shall be given unto you." And it was in the Sermon on the Mount that Jesus said, "Seek ye first the kingdom of God, and his righteousness; and all these things shall be added unto you" (Mt. 6:33). The Lord has set the priorities: God above self.

After we have accurately used our stewardship to please the Master, a portion is allocated for our necessities. Most Christians have this part backwards. They use their wages to provide for themselves, and then give if any is left over. But the question must be asked, "How much ought to be given?"

Years ago, it was a very popular thing to take a "vow of poverty." The German reformer, Martin Luther took such a vow during his college years.[1] Many believed that in taking such a vow, they would earn God's favor. There are two things wrong with this belief: first, it makes an erroneous parallel between wealth and sin. Second, it is unbiblical. You cannot earn God's favor through any work of your own! Grace is a free gift based upon Christ's meritorious sacrifice (Eph. 2:8-9). Salvation is not bequeathed to us through our giving back to God the stewardship He bestowed upon us in the first place.

Here is the line of demarcation; What is a need, what is a want, and how do I determine how to spend? Going back to the house discussed earlier, my wife and I determined through counsel and prayer that we needed a house to fulfil the ministry God has given to us. But which house, and how much of our monthly budget would be designated toward that need?

The same could be said for a car. Because I am a pastor, I often transport people to and from church, and to ministry opportunities. I also make frequent visits to hospitals, to retirement homes, to visit those who are in need of salvation or some other spiritual counsel, or to new homes for the purpose of witnessing. It is a need that I have a vehicle, but what type of vehicle should I get?

I must admit that I have not always made the right decision about purchasing a car. When in college, the Lord provided to me, through two generous men, a gift of $2,000 to purchase a car. Even in those days, $2,000 would not buy very much of a car. I decided (without truly seeking counsel) that I would borrow an additional $1,000, and spend $600 I had already saved, to purchase a used 2003 Red Pontiac Sunfire. It was a fun little car. It could go fast. I drove that car for six weeks before I wrecked it.

It was very discouraging to have wrecked that car I loved. I knew God had taken it away from me. The Lord was gracious unto me, and I received an insurance payout for $3,000 after my deductible. I paid back the $1,000 I borrowed, and was left with the $2,000 given to me six weeks earlier. This time, I sought the Lord in prayer, and wouldn't you know it, I bought a 1997 Pontiac Sunfire for $2,000. It was not red. It was a dirt-colored gold with sun blistered spots. It had only a few more miles on it than the first car.

I drove that Sunfire for five years, put 203,000 miles on the car, and God took care of me and it. I used that car to transport college students to work. I used it to bring others with me to ministry opportunities, and it was a wonderful car. The funniest thing about that whole story was that the car had been for sale since I purchased the first car, but I had overlooked it because I wanted something newer and shinier.

Staying in your budget is only hard when you can't determine needs from wants, or when you are lazy (we'll talk about that later). If you will do what God wants you to do, God will provide for your needs, but if you squander the Lord's resources, then you will lack. Remember the parable of the talents:

> *Take therefore the talent from him, and give it unto him which hath ten talents. For unto everyone that hath shall be given, and he shall have abundance: but from him that hath not shall be taken away even that which he hath. And cast ye the unprofitable servant into outer darkness: there shall be weeping and gnashing of teeth. (Mt. 25:28-30)*

STEWARDSHIP PRINCIPLE #5
When my stewardship is right, God may also provide abundance.

God has promised to provide for all our needs as we diligently, prayerfully, and carefully take care of His stewardship (Phil. 4:19). Sometimes, God will even go beyond our needs, and supply some of our wants! He does this because He is a good God, and as in the parable of the talents, He chooses to reward those who are faithful.

Not all rewards will be in this life. Most rewards will be reaped in the life to come. But there will be rewards for those who faithfully administer their stewardship. When the Lord returns, He will reward those who are faithful.

For we must all appear before the judgment seat of Christ; that every one may receive the things done in his body, according to that he hath done, whether it be good or bad. (2 Cor. 5:10)

If God chooses to bless with abundance in this life, how are we to treat this new abundance? Remember, it is still a stewardship.

Everyone enjoys vacations, right? Wrong. A few years back, my wife and I went on a vacation. We took a cruise to the Bahamas. It was the worst vacation I have ever taken. It was boring. I felt like I had wasted a lot of money. It was the first time I had gone abroad without being on a mission trip. I wanted to go find a missionary and be a help to them.

Since that trip, we have taken two international vacations, both of which were specifically to help missionaries. One trip to Brazil, and one trip to El Salvador. At the time of this writing we also are looking forward to two more trips abroad to El Salvador and India. These vacations are to help missionaries spread the Gospel!

What I have discovered is that my idea of a vacation is different now. The abundance God gives me, I still want to spend wisely as a steward. I enjoy travelling. I've been to ten foreign countries so far, and looking to add more, but I don't want to "waste" the travel on a vacation, I want to use it for God as a good steward.

You may be thinking I'm crazy. There is nothing wrong with going to Disneyland if God gives you the abundance to do it. But make sure you are still being wise as a steward! If God gives you $1,000 abundance for vacation, and a Disney cruise for the family costs $5,000, then don't waste the stewardship. You may need to set that money aside for a few years before you have enough of an abundance for such a trip, or you may choose to do something a little cheaper.

Many finance books talk a lot about debt (and we will talk about that later). I believe most Christians get into debt problems when they think their income is all theirs. They spend it on the abundance they want, and as a result they waste God's provision for their necessities. Then, they must take on debt to pay for their needs, because they squandered the talent God provided.

Make a budget. Organize according to God's plan, prioritizing what is good, better, and best. Diligently care for the stewardship provided to you by giving, spending, saving and investing according to what God would have you to do. Don't splurge on your wants unless God provides a blessing of abundance above the normal stewardship.

CHAPTER 2

Money is a Tool, not a Purpose

But they that will be rich fall into temptation and a snare, and into many foolish and hurtful lusts, which drown men in destruction and perdition. For the love of money is the root of all evil: which while some coveted after, they have erred from the faith, and pierced themselves through with many sorrows. (1 Tim. 6:9-10)

Money is not the root of all evil. It is the "love of money" that is the root of all evil. Money is just a tool. In the hand of a Christian who understands stewardship, it is an amazing force for good. But that same money in the hand of a backslidden, covetous Christian will pierce their heart with many sorrows.

What Is my purpose?

Everyone needs a purpose. Living up in the Northwest, we have long, dreary winters. You leave for work in the morning while it is dark, and you return when it is dark. This leads to a condition called SAD, Seasonal Affective Disorder. SAD is basically depression caused by lack of vitamin D, because we don't see the sun enough. Depression can be one of the most difficult disorders to combat. People who are not depressed tell you to just get over it. "Don't get down, get excited." "Don't be a pessimist, be an optimist."

I am naturally an optimist, but even being an optimist, sometimes life can feel like a hamster wheel, especially during the winter months. Wake up, go to work, get home and go to sleep. Repeat six days a week, and on my day off, find work to do around the house.

There are several conditions that help a person overcome depression. Diet, exercise, restful sleep, and friendly company all play an important role. But the most important (non-chemical) aspect to overcoming depression is purpose. What reason do you have for getting out of bed? What reason do I have for going to work? What reason do I have for spending God's money as a faithful steward?

Accumulating money is not a good goal. Accumulating things, or experiences, is not a good goal. The Bible calls that covetousness. The question must be, "Why do you accumulate wealth?"

I was speaking with a friend right before the Covid-19 shutdowns. We were talking about his goals. His goal was to accumulate $10 million. I asked him why. His response was so that he did not have to work anymore. But why? When the Covid-19 pandemic came to our area, he lost both his jobs. He did not work anymore. You know what he wanted to do? Get back to work so he would get back to saving and investing to get him back on his path to retirement.

There has to be a greater "Why" than simply "to not have to work anymore." Accumulating wealth is pointless without a plan for that wealth.

I have another friend with whom I attended college. We usually get together about four times a year. Last year in January we discussed our New Year's resolutions and goals. I was shocked when he told me that he and his wife had set 120 goals the previous year, and had successfully hit ninety of those goals. I had only set a measly twenty goals, and might have hit half of them.

I asked him how he had even kept track of the goals. He and his wife had made lists of goals: family goals, house goals, goals for the children, ministry goals, work goals, personal development goals, and just about every other category you could think of. They wrote every goal down, and every Saturday he and his wife reviewed their goals and asked what progress they had made.

Money was not the goal. Paying down the house to eliminate mortgage insurance was the goal. This would free up an extra $100 a month in their budget so they could give to a special project, or to use in some other way for God's glory. If money is your purpose and your goal, then you are aiming way too low.

I have a retirement goal. My goal in retirement is to travel the world, helping missionaries share the gospel of Jesus Christ. I want to go to a new country every month, fully self-supported, and be a blessing to missionaries. I want to hear about a missionary need, and write a check for $10,000 to cover that need, and do it whenever the Lord lays that burden on my heart. Retirement is not the goal, money is not the goal. I have a goal toward which I am working: that goal is to glorify God through missions.

According to an analysis conducted by Oregon State University of all the data collected from the 1992-2010 "Healthy Retirement Study," those who work to older ages live longer.[2] The number one hypothesis for why this is true has to do with purpose. When people lose their purpose, they lose their motivation. They eat less healthy food, or more food because their time is not regulated the same. They watch more TV instead of being active because they have more time to kill. Many get depressed because they have no purpose. (Pr. 29:18, "Where there is no vision, the people perish").

The Bible gives us purpose. We do not live unto ourselves, we live unto God (Rom. 14:7-8)! Solomon was one of the richest men to ever live. He was the richest king in all the Bible. He had wealth, power, wisdom, prestige, women and pleasure. How did it turn out for Solomon?

> *Vanity of vanities, saith the Preacher* [that is Solomon], *vanity of vanities; all is vanity. What profit hath a man of all his labour which he taketh under the sun? (Ecc. 1:2-3)*

The book of Ecclesiastes then goes on to list all the things Solomon pursued. All the goals he looked toward. What was Solomon's purpose?

1. <u>Solomon Gave His Heart to Seek Wisdom</u>

> *And I gave my heart to seek and search out by wisdom concerning all things that are done under heaven: this sore travail hath God given to the sons of man to be exercised therewith. I have seen all the works that are done under the sun; and, behold, all is vanity and vexation of spirit. (Ecc. 1:13-14)*

> *I communed with mine own heart, saying, Lo, I am come to great estate, and have gotten more wisdom than all they that have been before me in Jerusalem: yea, my heart had great experience of wisdom and knowledge. And I gave my heart to know wisdom, and to know madness and folly: I perceived that this also is vexation of spirit. For in much wisdom is much grief: and he that increaseth knowledge increaseth sorrow. (Ecc. 1:16-18)*

After searching diligently for knowledge and wisdom, Solomon found it was an empty purpose. No matter how much you learn, there are always more questions. And no matter how much you think you know, you still cannot solve the problems of our world. It is honorable to read books, to go to college and study, and to increase in knowledge, but knowledge and wisdom are empty purposes.

Recently I was at the hospital to visit a friend. While I was there, I saw a friend from high school. I had not seen him in ten years. We started talking about what he was doing. He was still a student at college getting another degree. He was pursuing a doctorate in mathematics. Why? So that he could spend his life attempting to solve math problems. He did not want to be a professor, though he likely would become a professor to pay the bills. His whole goal was to discover the mysteries of math.

Unfortunately, he was divorced and rarely saw his daughter. He was no longer in church. He was living the shallow and empty life of a lost man. In his pursuit of knowledge, he found life to be empty. He still clings to the hope that this pursuit will bring fulfillment. Some days it probably does, but it is an empty purpose.

2. <u>Solomon Then Sought Pleasure and Laughter</u>

> *I said in mine heart, Go to now, I will prove thee with mirth, therefore enjoy pleasure: and, behold, this also is vanity. (Ecc. 2:1)*

You would think that seeking happiness would make you happy, but Solomon found otherwise. Seeking happiness only made him realize just how empty he really was. Anyone can put on a smile and look satisfied with life, but jovial activity does not necessarily make for a joyous heart.

Our world today calls this hedonism; the pursuit of whatever pleases me. There are even many Christians who follow the tenets of hedonism. Attending religious services gives them a warm fuzzy feeling inside, so they attend. But then during football season, watching the Seattle Seahawks play gives them euphoria, so they do that instead. Then their wife is mad at them for not going to church, and if they make their wife happy, they'll have a happy life, so they record the game and go back to church.

I'm the type who loves to entertain (given to hospitality). I would have people over to my house every day of the week if my wife would let me. I love the jovial nature of friends playing games. But laughter is not a worthy goal. You can laugh all you want and still be empty on the inside. Pleasure does not provide purpose.

3. Solomon Then Tried Beauty

> *I made me great works; I builded me houses; I planted me vineyards: I made me gardens and orchards, and I planted trees in them of all kind of fruits: I made me pools of water, to water therewith the wood that bringeth forth trees. (Ecc. 2:4-6)*

Having the most beautiful house, escaping to the most beautiful vacation spots, and collecting the most beautiful artwork will still leave you empty. You can spend your wealth on all the beauty you can afford, but it will still leave you without purpose.

I know a man who greatly desires a piece of artwork by a particular artist. The artist produces custom pieces for individuals starting at around $125,000 each. This man will likely purchase a piece for his new home being built at the time of this writing. He will have a beautiful home, beautiful artwork, beautiful cars and watches and other accessories, and there is nothing wrong with possessing nice things, but none of them will bring satisfaction. You may work your whole life pursuing that goal, but discover, as Solomon did, that it is vanity.

4. <u>Solomon Tried Accumulating Wealth</u>

I gathered me also silver and gold, and the peculiar trea-
sure of kings and of the provinces…Then I looked on all
the works that my hands had wrought, and on the labour
that I had labored to do: and, behold, all was vanity and
vexation of spirit, and there was no profit under the sun.
(Ecc. 2:8,11)

If you make accumulating money your purpose, it may give you something to work toward, but it will deliver no satisfaction or fulfillment. It is an empty pursuit. After years of useless search, Solomon finally came to the conclusion that there is only one goal and purpose worth pursuing: God!

Let us hear the conclusion of the whole matter: fear God,
and keep his commandments: for this is the whole duty
of man. (Ecc. 12:13)

How Do I Use My Tool?

Money can be a very tangible way to measure many of your goals. This is where your budget is vital. Once you know your purpose, then you can budget to reach your purpose. God is my number one goal and purpose. He is the Master, I am the steward. What does He want me to do with my life, and how can I use the tool of money to accomplish that purpose?

If I believe God wants me to adopt a child and raise that child for His glory, then I can make a budget and use the tool of money to work toward that goal! I may set a three-year target goal for $20,000 to adopt. That works out to $555.55 per month as a line item in my budget to reach that goal. Money then becomes a tool to fulfill God's purpose for my life.

I may believe God wants me to help missionaries around the world preach the Gospel. I then create a line item in my budget of $250 per month to send to missionaries to help them on their way. Money becomes a tool to fulfill God's purpose for my life.

I may believe God wants me to one day give a $1,000,000 donation to my alma mater to build a building. So I determine to invest $1,000 per month into higher risk accounts averaging 10 percent annual growth. If that investment performs as expected, after twenty-three years, those investments will be worth $1,000,000, which I could then give for that purpose. Money becomes a tool I can use to achieve God's purpose for my life. Once I know God's purpose for me, I can use the tools He's given me to reach that purpose.

My wife and I have a category in our budget called "long term savings." This is money we will likely be using within the next one to three years. Anything longer than that, I deposit into an investment account of some sort. (Usually stocks for me, but could be CDs, bonds, or just a high yield savings account). Within our "long term savings" we have seven line items: Emergency Fund, Baby Fund, El Salvador Missions Trip, India Missions Trip, College Fund, Car Fund, and Taxes. You may have your own line items that will be different than mine. But once you know your purpose, you can create your budget.

We believe God wants us to set aside money for emergencies (we'll talk about that later), so we have a line item for emergencies. We believe God wants us to have children, so we have a line item budgeting for the medical expenses associated with having children. We believe God wants us to go help missionaries in El Salvador and India, so we have line items for each. And we believe God wants us to plan for when our car dies (we'll discuss cars later), so we have a line item for a replacement car. We also believe God wants us to pay the taxes we owe (we'll discuss taxes later). We then use the tools God has given to us (our paychecks, and any additional money God provides) to work toward our God-given goals.

Every dollar needs a designation. I mentioned earlier that I have forty-two line items in my budget. Every dollar that comes in gets allocated to one of these categories. For my consistent income (salaried paychecks) there is a set amount for each category. For inconsistent income (speaking engagements, side jobs, increased portfolio performance, etc.), these all still get allocated into whichever line items we feel we need to boost.

Some parts of the budget are consistently the same amount, other line items vary. My mortgage payment is the same month to month, but our utility costs vary based upon our gas and electric usage. After working out the expected monthly costs, I consistently apply an equal amount into my account month to month. That way a surplus accumulates during the lower usage months and is available during the higher usage months. The same is true for car maintenance, medical bills, and gas costs. The money is there when I need it, because I consistently adhere to my budget.

Covetousness leads to wicked actions.

Covetousness is a sin. It is clearly defined as something God hates. It was even included in the Ten Commandments, and is one of only two commands that deals with the heart (the other being to have no other gods before the Lord). Covetousness can be a hidden sin, but it is the root to many other sins. Why does someone steal? Because they covet. Why does someone commit adultery? Because of covetousness. And as 1 Timothy 6:10 states, it often will lead someone away from God.

> But they that will be rich fall into temptation and a snare, and into many foolish and hurtful lusts, which drown men in destruction and perdition. For the love of money is the root of all evil: which while some coveted after, they have erred from the faith, and pierced themselves through with many sorrows. (1 Tim. 6:9-10)

Not all covetousness looks the same. There are three major outfits that covetousness can wear. They manifest differently, but are all the same.

1. <u>Complaining</u>

The first and probably most obvious outfit that covetousness will wear is complaining. If I complain that my car is not as nice as his car, or I complain that my house is not as nice as his house, or I complain that my wife is not as good a cook as his wife, all of these are the manifestation of a covetous heart. Complaining is a condemnation against God that I deserve better than He has chosen to give me. It is effectively saying that God is not fair, or that God is not wise. That is why the Lord hates complaining.

Do all things without murmurings and disputings. (Phil. 2:14)

The Children of Israel, during their exodus wanderings, were constantly complaining. God parted the Red Sea so they could walk across on dry ground, and destroyed the Egyptians behind them. There was celebration for two days before the complaining began. They were thirsty, and did not trust God to provide water (Ex. 15:22-24). Their complaining was covetousness. They wanted something they did not have.

Water is essential for life, so you might easily suggest that the Israelites had every right to complain. You might suggest that their complaining was not covetousness, it was genuine need. The need was there, but the attitude was covetousness. They had no faith. They should have gone to God in prayer, but instead they murmured.

You might give the Israelites a pass in this instance because they really did not yet know God. They were slaves recently set free. God met the need because it was a genuine need, but only four weeks later, a similar thing happened. Israel was in the wilderness, and water was scarce. They should have trusted that God would take care of the need as He had done a month earlier, but instead, they got mad at Moses!

Wherefore the people did chide with Moses, and said, Give us water that we may drink. And Moses said unto them, Why chide ye with me? Wherefore do ye tempt the LORD? And the people thirsted there for water; and the people murmured against Moses, and said, Wherefore is this that

thou hast brought us up out of Egypt, to kill us and our
children and our cattle with thirst? (Ex. 17:2-3)

The genuine need had arisen for water, but the heart was not right. The spirit of covetousness overwhelmed their miniscule faith. They forgot God's previous blessings in favor of their current circumstance. The spirit of covetousness led to complaining. Moses said they were tempting the Lord.

Both of these circumstances were genuine needs, but the spirit of covetousness led to complaining rather than praying. You might give the Israelites a pass (even though the Lord did not) because they had genuine need, but the spirit of complaining went far beyond their needs. God provided the Israelites with food from heaven every day called manna. It was savory, tasting like the coriander seed. It could be ground and baked into cakes, and tasted like fresh oil. But Israel complained about God's provision.

We remember the fish, which we did eat in Egypt freely;
the cucumbers, and the melons, and the leeks, and the
onions, and the garlick: But now our soul is dried away:
there is nothing at all, beside this manna, before our eyes.
(Num. 11:5-6)

Now the spirit of complaining was very evident. Their circumstance was infinitely better following God than it had been as slaves in Egypt, but their covetous hearts were blinded. Look at what they said:

a. The Food We Did Freely Eat

Israel had a skewed view of how things had been. They had been slaves! Why did they have fish to eat? Because it was the cheapest meat. And as slaves, I'm sure they were not given the best fish to eat. They were likely given the leftovers. Then they described all the vegetables accessible in Egypt. Again, they were not given the best, they were slaves.

They also reveal their skewed perception of the past. They said that in Egypt they did eat "freely." No they didn't! They were slaves. They were told when to eat, what to eat, and when they had had enough to eat. Nothing they did was "freely." But they overlooked those details, because the heart of covetousness is always focused elsewhere.

b. Our Soul Is Dried Away

Israel complained that the manna was killing their spirit. They were falling into depression because of the manna. The manna had nothing to do with their spirit. It was just their "straw-man" argument to detract from their own sin of covetousness. Their soul was actually "drying away" because they were not on the Lord's side, as was evidenced by their actions at Mt. Sinai (Exodus 32).

There are a good many people in our country, and in our churches, who struggle with depression, bitterness, and envy. Like a cancer, it is eating away at them from the inside out. They may point to unfulfilled expectations, or someone letting them down, as the source of their spiritual wilderness, but the root is often a form of covetousness.

c. There Is Nothing At All Beside This Manna

If it were true that they only had manna to eat, it still would have been sufficient, because it was God's divine gift of sustaining bread. But it was not true! God promised He would supply meat for Israel, and Moses asked this question:

Shall the flocks and the herds be slain for them, to suffice them? Or shall all the fish of the sea be gathered together for them, to suffice them? (Num. 11:22)

This statement of Moses makes two things evidently clear: first, they had flocks and herds. They could eat them if they chose to eat them. Second, they were close enough to the sea that they could gather fish if they wanted. Israel's complaint was that there was "nothing at all beside this manna." Their complaining spirit blinded them to the resources at hand.

When the Lord called Moses to serve Him, Moses gave excuses. God dispelled all his excuses and asked Moses, "What is that in thine hand?" (Ex. 4:2) There is a principle we can learn from this and many other passages in the Bible. God will always give you what you need to succeed in the work He has called you to do.

Elijah went forty days into the wilderness in the strength of a divine meal. Noah was given 120 years to build the ark before God's judgment fell. David needed only a sling and five smooth stones to conquer the enemy of God. Gideon only needed 300 warriors, and some lamps to overcome a multitude of enemies. The widow of Zarephath had only a handful of meal and a little oil. When you know your purpose, then look for what God has already given you to fulfill that purpose.

When it comes to the stewardship God has bestowed upon us, complaining is like a slap in the face to God. It is essentially saying that God has been unfair to grant us such a small stewardship.

2. Impulsive Spending

Covetousness will often reveal itself in impulsive spending, or stealing. Our society runs on impulse. According to *Magnifymoney.com*, Americans averaged $1,325 in Christmas debt in 2019.[3] That is $1,325 spent more than they could afford on Christmas items. Did you know that Christmas happens every year? So why did it catch consumers by surprise? It didn't, they just did not know how to control their impulsive spending.

I'm an impulsive spender too. The other day I needed some pants. I walked into the store and saw their sales. I walked out with two new pairs of pants and three new shirts. Unlike many, I had the funds available in the budget line item of "clothes" to cover the cost. But the shirts were still impulse purchases. I saw them, I wanted them, and I purchased them.

Most impulse purchasing is a result of covetousness. You see something that you just can't live without, so you figure out a way to purchase that item, even if it means going into debt. Often, you may go to purchase a need, and walk out with a want. You go in to purchase pants you needed and come out having purchased shirts you wanted.

Impulse spending, for many, is the largest reason they are poor. If God gives you a stewardship, and you squander that stewardship impulsively, then why should God trust you with a greater supply? It should be no surprise that many Christians give less in the summer months.[4] They squandered the stewardship on impulsive vacations.

Worse than impulsive spending is impulsive stealing. Stealing from a store, stealing from a boss, or stealing from the Lord is usually a result of covetousness. This is why the love of money is the root of all kinds of evil.

One of the best-known parables Jesus gave is that of the Prodigal Son. "Prodigal" means to "spend money or resources freely and recklessly; wastefully extravagant." There was a father with two sons. The younger had a heart of covetousness, and it built up within him day after day. Eventually that covetousness led to such resentment toward his father that he wished his father was dead.

And the younger of them said to his father, Father, give
me the portion of goods that falleth to me... (Lk. 15:2)

This boy was more concerned with the resources of his father than he was for the man. The boy's disrespect said, "I wish you were dead so that I might have my inheritance now." This type of covetousness led to short-term impulsive spending and waste. The young man "YOLO'd" away his inheritance. Then, when a famine came, he was left destitute, because he never controlled his impulsive spending.

While I was in Bible college, I worked a secular job in a warehouse. Some of my co-workers lived life with this philosophy. YOLO (You Only Live Once) means that you live for today. Often I would hear stories of the drunken debauchery in which these lost souls participated. It amazed me that someone would work all week long to earn $600 so they could blow $200 of it on alcohol over the weekend! It was short-term impulsive covetousness. They wanted the party lifestyle at the expense of their future prosperity.

3.   Long-Term Frivolous Saving

The third outfit that covetousness may wear seems more like wise saving, but it isn't. You can be wise financially, but still consumed with covetousness. You long for the red Ferrari sports car, so you diligently save every penny you can save for five years and then purchase the car with cash. You were not unwise in your finances. You were frugal and disciplined, and you had a goal. But your goal was frivolous; nothing more than covetousness.

There is a growing movement among the Millennial Generation called FIRE: Financial Independence Retire Early. This movement has many fantastic, and even biblical, financial ideas. But the one negative catalyst is often covetousness. Why retire early? So I can have the lifestyle I want to have. There is a goal, there is a purpose, and there is discipline to achieve that purpose. Unfortunately, many of these FIRE followers are chasing the wrong purpose. Like Solomon, their pursuits are vanity, because they do not pursue God!

Whether it is long-term disciplined saving for a TV, for a car, or for that once-in-a-lifetime vacation, if your purpose is anything other than pleasing God, the purpose will be vanity. It is nothing more than long-term covetousness. And covetousness leads to all types of evil.

But godliness with contentment is great gain. For we brought nothing into this world, and it is certain we can carry nothing out. And having food and raiment let us be therewith content. (1 Tim. 6:6-8)

There is nothing wrong with saving for a car, vacation, or nicer house. In fact, if you are going to acquire these items, you need to save for them in your budget. But none of these things will produce godliness, and nothing is really gained. Contentment brings godliness, and the two together are great gain! There are many things far more valuable than what can be purchased with finances.

a. A Virtuous Wife — *Proverbs 31:10, Who can find a virtuous woman? For her price is far above rubies.*

b. The Holy Spirit's Power — *Acts 8:20, But Peter said unto him, Thy money perish with thee, because thou hast thought that the gift of God may be purchased with money.*

c. The Peace of God--*Philippians 4:6-7, Be careful for nothing; but in every thing by prayer and supplication with thanksgiving let your requests be made known unto God. And the peace of God, which passeth all understanding, shall keep your hearts and minds through Christ Jesus.*

d. Salvation from Sin — *Ephesians 2:8, For by grace are ye saved through faith; and that not of yourselves: it is the gift of God.*

There are a great many things we can save up to purchase, but they are all temporal. Find your purpose in God, and pursue Him. Then, all these other things will fall into their proper place (Mt. 6:33).

There was a man in the Bible named Gehazi who had a long-term frivolous savings plan. He wanted to purchase land, and houses. He wanted servants and singers. But his covetousness led him to despair. It began when a leprous general from Syria came to Elisha, the man of God, requesting to be healed. Elisha instructed him how to be clean. In return, General Naaman wanted to give a gift of gratitude to him, but the prophet refused the gift. Elisha did not need it, and did not believe God wanted him to take it. But Gehazi's covetousness led to deceit. He rode out after General Naaman.

> *But Gehazi, the servant of Elisha the man of God, said, Behold, my master hath spared Naaman the Syrian, in not receiving at his hands that which he brought: but, as the LORD liveth, I will run after him, and take somewhat of him. So Gehazi followed after Naaman. And when Naaman saw him running after him, he lighted down from the chariot to meet him, and said, Is all well? And he said, All is well. My master hath sent me, saying, Behold, even now there be come to me from mount Ephraim two young men of the sons of the prophets: give them, I pray thee, a talent of silver, and two changes of garments. (2 Kings 5:20-22)*

Gehazi's covetousness led to multiple lies, stealing from Naaman what did not belong to him, concealing the money in his own house, and pretending nothing had happened. Though Naaman never knew what had happened, God knew, and revealed to Elisha the covetous heart of Gehazi. The result was than Gehazi received the leprosy of Naaman upon himself, and he was thrust out from the presence of the man of God. He was no longer allowed to serve God.

You may get what you want through hard work and long-term savings, or you may get what you want through short-term thievery and dishonesty, but you will never achieve your purpose in God by seeking after things with a covetous heart.

It is more blessed to give than to receive.

> *I have shewed you all things, how that so laboring ye ought to support the weak, and to remember the words of the Lord Jesus, how he said, It is more blessed to give than to receive. (Acts 20:35)*

Nothing cures covetousness quicker than giving. The root of covetousness is the perceived happiness we will receive from the things we hope to acquire, but Jesus said it is more blessed (happy) to give than to receive. Money is a tool in our hand, and oftentimes, the best use for that tool is to fix someone else's problems.

I have a very nice set of tools. I purchased them when I purchased my home, because I had a lot of projects in the house (it was a fixer-upper). Those tools have not really brought me much enjoyment. They are just tools I use. The finished product has brought me enjoyment, but not the tools. The most enjoyment I receive from my tools now are when I either lend them out, or use them to help someone else with a project.

My brother-in-law was working to convert an open space in his basement into an office. I brought my tools over, and I helped him build that wall and frame in the new door. I received about as much joy and satisfaction out of that project as you could imagine possible. I was so proud of my tools, and how effective they were at performing the task. Using those tools to help someone else brought me more joy from those tools than having them sit in my garage.

When we think of giving, we usually first think of giving money, but the stewardship God has entrusted to us is far greater than money. God has entrusted us with time to spend wisely for Him. God has entrusted us with abilities to spend wisely for Him. God has entrusted us with knowledge we are to use wisely for Him. If you are a Bible-believing Christian, God has entrusted to you the Gospel message, which you are to spend for Him. Our lives are a stewardship given to us by God, and we are to generously and wisely give according to how He would have us to give!

As was mentioned several times already, if God entrusted me with $100 million to give away, I could easily find worthy causes for those funds. However, the question must be asked: What am I doing with the stewardship I do have? The important question is not how much you give, but how much you keep. It all belongs to God, so how much of God's money will I use to support myself?

At different stages of life, we may require different amounts of money to support ourselves and our families. I find it unfathomable that someone would spend $2,500 per month on health care, and yet that is what some require to continue living. My

$2,000 per month spent on housing seems outrageous to some who live in rural Georgia, and yet it is only a fraction of what it might cost to live in New York City, or downtown Los Angeles. So the dollar amount or the percentage will be different through different locations, and the budget will change through different stages of life. Each of us must examine our budgets, and seriously ask the question: "Does this line item amount please God for my situation?"

Recently, a Christian financial planner spoke at our church. He gave a few "rule of thumb" percentages for different expenses within a budget. I was shocked at his food budget. He suggested that the food budget should be no more than 20 percent of your take home pay. My wife and I did the math, and our food budget was 4 percent, only one-fifth the amount of his "rule of thumb." But then when he mentioned the housing expenses, our housing expense was close to double his "rule of thumb." It had nothing to do with being so poor we could not afford food. It was our stage of life. Having a home is more expensive in our area than the national average, and food is less expensive (as a percentage of income) than other parts of the country.

When it comes to giving, the same standard is applied. How much you give is not based upon your income, it is based upon your heart. Many Christians focus on the tithe (which we will discuss later), but they neglect the heart. Look at the story found in Luke 21.

> *And he looked up, and saw the rich men casting their gifts*
> *into the treasury. And he saw also a certain poor widow*
> *casting in thither two mites. And he said, Of a truth I say*
> *unto you, that this poor widow hath cast in more than*

they all: For all these have of their abundance cast in unto the offerings of God: but she of her penury hath cast in all the living that she had. (Lk. 21:1-4)

This story highlights the heart of giving. Giving for man's applause (as is often done today) results in nothing more than stroking the ego. But giving out of love results in the blessedness of which Jesus spoke. Even though the two farthings given were miniscule and insignificant, they were a sacrifice for the widow, who had a small stewardship. This gift was more important to her than even her own necessities, and she pleased the Father.

I can't tell you how many times I have been blessed by giving. I have saved for items only to have God lay upon my heart the need to give it away. Though sometimes it hurt to see my goal go back to zero, God always made up for it with some unexpected joy. He has taught me to hold loosely to the stuff I accumulate in this world, and give liberally from what He has provided to me. This is what stewards do; they allocate the resources of their master according to the master's desires. This will lead to the commendation, "Well done, thou good and faithful servant" (Mt. 25:21).

CHAPTER 3

Tithes, Offerings, and Non-Religious Giving

⚙️

W hen examining giving in the Bible, the common subject is that of the tithe. Pastors speak on the tithe because it is an easy, convenient "rule of thumb" to teach people to give. Unfortunately, many pastors inaccurately apply Old Testament passages on the tithe to suit their own convenient purposes. So, what was and is the tithe (from the Bible), and is it applicable in New Testament churches today?

History and Context of the Tithe

The word "tithe" means "tenth." It was always used to mean one tenth. There are many who inaccurately use the term to mean their regular general gift to their church, whether it is a tenth or not. I was told one time by a young Christian friend that he had been giving his $20 tithe every week. I was glad that he was consistently giving to the work of the Lord, but that is not a tithe. I happened to know that his weekly income was more than $200 per week. They were giving an offering to the Lord, but it was not a tithe.

Others have inaccurately stated that they give their tithe to their church every week, but are actually giving more than one tenth. This again is not a tithe. It is an offering, and I am glad that they have developed a heart of giving, but it is not a tithe. A tithe means a tenth.

When God delivered to the Jewish people His law, included in that law were the statutes needed for all areas of their lives. It included dietary restrictions, it included cleansing rituals, it included religious ceremony, it included domestic regulations for slaves, children, husbands and wives, and it also included how to fund certain political and religious needs. There are several different tithes mentioned in the Scriptures:

Abraham (before the law) gave a tithe of all the spoils of war from the conquest of King Chedorlaomer. Then he gave the rest back to the king of Sodom, saying that "I will not take from a thread even to a shoelatched" from the spoils of war (Gen. 14:23). This tithe given was not compulsory, it was not part of the law to God's people. It was a freewill thanksgiving offering for God's protection. Then upon giving the tenth, he gave the rest away too.

Jacob made a vow to God that if the Lord would do something for him, he would give a tithe back to God (Gen. 28:20-22). This type of vow is a foolish vow. God deserves our best, and our gifts, regardless of the level of His blessings upon us.

Then, in Leviticus 27, God gave the portion of the law to His people Israel concerning their giving of tithes. I say tithes (plural) because the law had more than one. There were three specific tithes, for three specific purposes given in the Law.

1. <u>Tithe on the Increase</u>

And all the tithe of the land, whether of the seed of the land, or of the fruit of the tree, is the LORD's: it is holy unto the LORD. (Lev. 27:30)

When the majority of people today think of a tithe, this is what they think about. Giving the increase of their possessions. It is also called a "heave offering" in the Bible. A "heave offering" comes from the Hebrew word transliterated *ter-oo-mow*, and means a tribute offering. It is God's tribute because He is in control. This heave offering was an annual tribute to God based on the increase from the year.

I have a friend who builds houses. He was concerned about tithing on a house he sold, because it would be such a large amount, and he needed to live on the proceeds from the sale of the house. I explained to him that if he was going to give a tithe, it would not be on the sale price, but on the profit (increase) of the house.

The tithe was on the increase. God did not demand continual tithes on the same provision year after year. There were other offerings in the Scriptures that were different, such as the offering given at the birth of a son, the census tax whenever the people were counted, or special levies to build or renovate the temple. None of these were tithes. The tithe (heave offering) was given annually on the increase.

Where did this money go? It did not go to the government. It did not go to feed the poor. It did not go to the United Way or some other social charity. It was specifically commanded of the Jews that it be given to the ministers of God, the priests and Levites.

> *But the tithes of the children of Israel, which they offer as an heave offering unto the LORD, I have given to the Levites to inherit... (Num. 18:24)*

The tribute to God was specifically to fund the ministry of God. The Levites were chosen by God to serve Him in the tabernacle, and later in the temple. If they were going to devote the majority of their life to serving God, then they would not have time to work the fields, or build, or sell wares. Service to God required all their attention and effort.

Interestingly, this tithe did not serve to build the tabernacle or the temple. It could not be used to build a building, because the tithe was given in the form of the harvest. If the Lord blessed an Israeli farmer with 10,000 apples, then 1,000 apples would be given as a heave offering. You can't build a temple out of apples. If the farmer thought it was too difficult to bring 1,000 apples to the temple, he could sell the apples and bring the money, but he was required to add the fifth part more. He'd sell 1,200 and bring the money to the temple. (Lev. 27:31)

2. Tithe for Religious Ceremonial Expenses

The second tithe was a "forced savings account." It required providing a tenth of the increase to bring to the temple during the Jewish feasts. It was theirs to consume during their required vacation.

And thou shalt eat before the LORD thy God, in the place which he shall choose to place his name there, the tithe of thy corn, of thy wine, and of thine oil, and the firstlings of thy herds and of they flocks; that thou mayest learn to fear the LORD thy God always. (Deut. 14:23)

Three times in a year shall all thy males appear before the LORD thy God in the place which he shall choose; in the feast of unleavened bread, and in the feast of weeks, and in the feast of tabernacles: and they shall not appear before the LORD empty. (Deut. 16:16)

God required His people to attend the temple ceremonies at least three times in a year. How could they afford to do that? How could they afford the journey, the cost of lodging, the cost of food, and all other costs associated with this required vacation? God required a tenth of their income be set aside for these trips. This tithe was not given to the temple (although God did tell them to remember the Levite as a part of this tithe), instead, this was for their expenses.

This tithe is almost never spoken about in our culture today. The Jews do not observe it, because they have no standing temple. Christian pastors don't mention it, because it does not particularly help their ministry.

We will discuss whether these tithes are necessary to the church later, but if this were to be accurately applied, it would definitely help the spread of the Gospel. Can you imagine if every family in your church set aside money so that they could take a vacation to help missionaries? Or if they took a week off of work to help run a Vacation Bible School? Or if they could take a week off of work to be a chaperone at a teen camp? The application of such a principle would greatly enhance the work of God!

3.   Tithe for the Poor

The third tithe was given to support the poor every third year. Many today call it alms giving.

> *At the end of three years thou shalt bring forth all the tithe of this increase the same year, and shalt lay it up within thy gates: And the Levite, (because he hath no part nor inheritance with thee,) and the stranger, and the father-less, and the widow, which are within thy gates, shall come, and shall eat and be satisfied; that the LORD thy God may bless thee in all the work of thine hand which thou doest. (Deut. 14:28)*

The third tithe was only given on the third year. It was not brought to the temple, but was for the local needs of their individual towns. It was brought to a common place in the town, stored, and dispersed for the needy over the next three years. The Levites in that local area had the charge of distributing to the needy, including themselves.

This might be equivalent today to giving a portion to local charities such as the Salvation Army, which works to provide shelter for the homeless, and food for the hungry. By the numbers, America is the most charitable country in terms of donating money to such causes.[5] That giving only accounted for a grand total of 1.44 percent of GDP in 2016 (GDP is the Gross Domestic Product, or total monetary value of all goods and services produced within a country during a year). This giving was nearly double the next highest country in charitable donation (Canada, at 0.77 percent of GDP). Can you imagine the help that could be provided if that number increased to the 10 percent every third year, as God commanded Israel to give?

4. Other Forms of Giving

The tithes were not the only offerings the Jews gave. There were also free will offerings. Sometimes, the free will offerings were more than enough!

> *And they spake unto Moses, saying, The people bring much more than enough for the service of the work, which the LORD commanded to make. And Moses gave commandment, and they caused it to be proclaimed throughout the camp, saying, Let neither man nor woman make any more work for the offering of the sanctuary. So the people were restrained from bringing. For the stuff they had was sufficient for all the work to make it, and too much. (Ex. 36:5-7)*

Giving is a way of life. It is more than just the line items in your budget, it is an attitude. Do you want to give? When God gives you a stewardship, it does not belong to you. When God has a purpose for that money, give cheerfully, not grudgingly (Mt. 12:35).

Application of the Tithe Today

Many churches and pastors preach and teach on tithing. While tithing does predate the law given by Moses, nowhere in the New Testament is the church commanded to bring a tithe. Instead, the church is commanded to give "as God has prospered us" (1 Cor. 16:2), and "according to his ability" (Acts 11:29) and "cheerfully" (2 Cor. 9:7), and of a "willing mind" (2 Cor. 8:12). In fact, the only time tithes are mentioned in the New Testament are when Jesus condemned the Pharisees for their hypocrisy (Mt. 23:23), and when speaking of the Old Testament patriarchs (Hebrews 7).

There are several important reasons why tithing is not a command to the church.

1. The Church is Not Israel

Many pastors may resist this claim, but the truth is that the Church is not the same as Israel. God gave different commands to Israel than He did the Church. Christians are not under the law, but under grace, and this applies to **all** of the law.

> But if ye be led of the Spirit, ye are not under the law. (Gal. 5:18)

> Every man according as he purposeth in his heart, so let him give; not grudgingly, or of necessity [forcibly as by the law]: for God loveth a cheerful giver. (2 Cor. 9:7)

> But there rose up certain of the sect of the Pharisees which believed, saying, That it was needful to circumcise them, and to command them to keep the law of Moses... Now therefore why tempt ye God, to put a yoke upon the neck of the disciples, which neither our fathers nor we were able to bear? (Acts 15:5, 10)

Christians are under no scriptural obligation to be circumcised. Christians are under no scriptural obligation to keep the Sabbath. Christians are under no scriptural obligation to keep the dietary laws of the Jews. Christians are under no scriptural obligation to present themselves three times a year to the temple. And Christians are under no scriptural obligation to give the Old Testament tithes.

God has made a distinction between His covenant with Israel (the Old Covenant), and his covenant with the Church (the New Covenant). Paul even went so far as to call the Old Covenant components "weak and beggarly elements" (Gal. 4:9-10).

There are far-reaching implications to this truth of separation between Israel and the Church. It solidifies our understanding of Eschatology [study of end-time prophecies]. It confirms our exegesis on Soteriology [study of salvation]. It is the foundation for the American idea of "Separation of Church and State." Israel was a portrayal of God's righteousness and justice, the Church is a portrayal of Christ's love, mercy and grace.

2. <u>In the Church, Everyone is a Minister</u>

The Israelites essentially paid the Levites to minister before God. It was their inheritance. And the tithe provided to the Levites the financial ability to serve God. But in the church, every member is a minister. Every born again child of God has access to the Throne of Grace (Heb. 4:16). We all offer spiritual sacrifices before God.

> *Ye also, as lively stones, are built up a spiritual house, an*
> *holy priesthood, to offer up spiritual sacrifices, acceptable*
> *to God by Jesus Christ. (1 Pet. 2:5)*

The Old Testament law did require the Levites to give tithes on their collected tithes (Num. 18:26), but the point remains that if the New Testament church is under the Jewish commands of the law, every member would be eligible to receive tithes. The tithes went to the Levites, not just to the priests. In the New Testament church, every member is a minister, and thereby equivalent to the Levites of the law.

3. The Holy Spirit's law in our hearts is more personal than the Law of Moses

The Holy Spirit of God dwells inside every believer. We are not bound under the law, we are under grace, and as such, the tithe (as described in the law) is not required. Instead, the Holy Spirit of God will reveal to you how to give, when to give, and how much to give. He may even use this book to guide you into practical applications of giving. Since the Spirit of God dwells in us, we have the freedom to follow His leading.

Some might quickly think in their hearts that they are now free from giving. But I point you back to the first chapter. We are stewards of God's resources. It does not belong to us anyway. The true test is: Will we be faithful stewards? Don't let covetousness or greed sway your mindset away from generosity, because God loves a cheerful giver. As a steward of God's resources, do what God loves!

Giving Strategies

If the tithe is not required, how should we give? Though the New Testament never commands Christians to give tithes, it does require that Christians give offerings. So, what are those offerings, when should we give them, and how much should we give?

1. <u>What Offerings Do We Give?</u>

Every offering recorded in Scripture after the death of Jesus Christ is a free will offering or an alms offering. But the free will offerings seem to take on the role the tithe (heave offering) previously fulfilled.

> *Do ye not know that they which minister about the holy things live of the things of the temple? And they which wait at the altar are partakers with the altar? Even so hath the Lord ordained that they which preach the gospel should live of the gospel. (1 Cor. 9:13-14)*

Paul compares the method of supporting the priests in the temple with the method of supporting those who preach the gospel. The priests lived off the gifts to God. In the same way, those who preach the Gospel ought to live off the gifts brought to the church. It does not say how much should be brought (we'll save that for later), but it is very clear that pastors derive their livelihood from the gifts of the church members. This is reiterated in 1 Timothy 5:17-18.

> *Let the elders that rule well be counted worthy of double honour, especially they who labour in the word and doctrine. For the scripture saith, Thou shalt not muzzle the*

> *ox that treadeth out the corn. And, The labourer is worthy*
> *of his reward. (1 Tim. 5:17-18)*

If the pastor labors earnestly for the Lord in the Word and doctrine, than his financial supply ought to be provided by the gifts to the church.

There are other offerings to be given to the New Testament Church as well. Not all the gifts go to provide financially for the pastors and rulers. Some offerings given to the church are to be used to help other brethren in the church.

> *And the multitude of them that believed were of one heart*
> *and of one soul: neither said any of them that ought of*
> *the things which he possessed was his own; but they had*
> *all things common... And Joses... Having land, sold it,*
> *and brought the money, and laid it at the apostles' feet.*
> *(Acts 4:32, 37)*

The early Christians freely gave to support one another financially. At the time, the church was located exclusively in Jerusalem, and many of the new converts lived in other cities. They were staying in Jerusalem to learn more from the apostles, but they needed food to eat, a place to sleep, and possibly other things. So, a free will offering was given by many, including Joses (who is Barnabas), so that these new believers could stay and learn and grow.

These same "free will" offerings were used to take care of the widows. All the Jews were supposed to care for widows (as commanded by God in their three-year tithe), but many would not. Even among those who seemed to be religious (such as the

Pharisees), many chose to ignore the widows of the community, or even their own needy parents. Some of the Pharisees had declared "Corban" upon their wealth, thus prohibiting them from caring for their parents financially ("Corban" will be discussed later under "Wasted Giving"). The church was different! The church understood that caring for widows and fatherless was a true sign of piety!

> *Pure religion and undefiled before God and the Father is this, To visit the fatherless and widows in their affliction, and to keep himself unspotted from the world. (Jms. 1:27)*

In Acts 6, there were so many widows in the church that it required a lot of work (and cost) to ensure they were cared for properly. It became a task too heavy for only the apostles, and they had to choose (or appoint) seven men to take over the business of caring for widows. Most believe that these were the first deacons in the church. "Deacon" means "a servant." These servants used the church treasury to care for the needy.

On other occasions, we see that the church gave offerings to the Apostle Paul so that he might go and preach the gospel in new places. This would be called missions giving today.

> *I robbed other churches, taking wages of them, to do you service. And when I was present with you, and wanted, I was chargeable to no man: for that which was lacking to me the brethren which came from Macedonia supplied: and in all things I have kept myself from being burdensome unto you, and so will I keep myself. (2 Cor. 11:8-9)*

Paul took his support from the churches in Macedonia, so that he could serve in Corinth without needing to worry about financial provision. He called it "robbing other churches" because the Corinthian believers had not grown to the place of spiritual maturity where they would provide for their own pastor. It therefore became an act of robbery because those who could support their pastor would not.

There are many offerings that Christians could give. But we see that there are definitely a few offerings that Christians must give. They are: giving to support their spiritual leader, giving to support the needy around them, and giving to support the Gospel going to new places.

2. <u>When Do We Give?</u>

For the Jews, they were required to give alms every third year. This was not a tithe in which they saved 3.3 percent for three years and then gave. It was 10 percent of that third year. One gift every three years. They gave regular heave offerings at their harvest times. That was when they had the increase, so that was when they gave. For their pilgrimage offerings, they saved their increase so they might use it three times in the year. But when should Christians give?

> *Now concerning the collection for the saints, as I have given order to the churches of Galatia, even so do ye. Upon the first day of the week let every one of you lay by him in store, as God hath prospered him, that there be no gatherings when I come. (1 Cor. 16:1-2)*

Paul instructed all the churches of Galatia, and this church in Corinth, that they lay aside gifts weekly on the first day of the week. This was a collection that would be given to another church (at Jerusalem) to assist them, yet it was still given weekly. Why? So there was no mad rush to collect a big offering when Paul arrived. Some would not have been faithfully setting aside an offering in their budget. If they had waited, there would not be much they could give.

As a side note, the church was meeting upon the first day of the week, not on the Sabbath. This is further clarification that the Church and Israel are not the same. Israel worshiped, and gave, on the seventh day of the week (the Sabbath), but the church worships and gives on the first day of the week, in commemoration of Christ's resurrection. It was not the Catholic Church who "switched the Sabbath." It was the common practice of the earliest believers to meet and give on Sundays.

The Macedonian churches also give us a pattern of giving during hard times.

> *How that in a great trial of affliction the abundance of their joy and their deep poverty abounded unto the riches of their liberality. For to their power, I bear record, yea, and beyond their power they were willing of themselves; Praying us with much intreaty that we would receive the gift... (2 Cor. 8:2-4)*

I have heard many say that when they get a new job, or when the market improves, or when the kids are out of school, then they will give. But the obvious example of 2 Corinthians 8 is that you give consistently when the Lord prompts you to give. Do it then, don't wait!

In our modern era of technological advancements, it is easier than ever to give, but it is also easier than ever to forget to give. That is why you **must** have a budget, you must abide by your budget, and you must change your budget, if necessary, to satisfy the requests of the Holy Spirit when He speaks to your heart.

3. <u>How Much Should We Give?</u>

There is no New Testament standard for the amount we are to give. There is no dollar figure, no percentage, and no standard. Free will offerings are controlled by the Holy Spirit.

Recently, my wife and I experienced a financial setback. During this time, the Lord laid upon our hearts a newly married couple who had just lost their income. We did not have the money in our budget to give what the Spirit laid upon our hearts to give. It was (for us) a substantial gift, especially considering our financial setback. And yet in giving that gift in obedience to the Spirit's leading, the Lord returned to us all the funds we needed, and even supplied above the gift amount we gave in an unexpected investment return.

You cannot give too much if you follow the Lord's leading. But here are a few practical ways to start giving.

a. Commit to Give As the Lord Prospers You

> *Upon the first day of the week let every one of you lay by him in store, as God hath prospered him... (1 Cor. 16:2)*

This implies that you make a commitment to give a percentage of God's increase to the Lord through your local church. Because there is no clear standard for what that amount should be, it is up to you to listen to the voice of the Holy Spirit as He leads you. You may choose to do what the law required (a tithe), or you may choose to do more or less. But keep in mind that you are a steward of God's money. It is not your own.

There was a famous preacher years ago who became very wealthy through book deals and preaching engagements. Upon his death he had a negligibly small amount of wealth left behind to give to his children. Upon investigation it was discovered that for many decades he and his wife had been increasing their giving, until they were giving away over 90 percent of their income to the work of the Lord. Each year they determined to give just a little bit more, and God honored their stewardship by giving to them more to manage.

Years ago, I was told that if God required a tithe under the law, should He not deserve more under grace? If you are a born again child of God, your heavenly Father deserves everything you have. Don't let a spirit of covetousness spoil your giving. Remember what God said of Israel when they withheld their giving:

> Will a man rob God? Yet ye have robbed me. But ye say, Wherein have we robbed thee? In tithes and offerings. Ye are cursed with a curse: for ye have robbed me, even this whole nation. (Mal. 3:8-9)

If a tenth was the necessary amount to fund the work of God in Israel, surely a tenth is a good baseline for funding the work of God in the local church.

b. Commit to Give Sacrificially

Back to the story of the widow's two mites (Lk. 21:2). Jesus was most pleased with her gift because it was given out of sacrifice. When Paul received the gift from the churches of Macedonia, it was with honor and some reluctance that he received it, for it was also given out of sacrifice. This principle goes back to the Old Testament when King David said, "I will not offer to the Lord that which doth cost me nothing" (2 Sam. 24:24).

Sacrificial giving does not require that you be poor your whole life, nor does it imply that you blow your whole budget and just trust God. If your sacrificial giving is prompted by the Holy Spirit (and not by a persuasive televangelist), then God will be certain to make up any shortfall to ensure your needs are met (Phil. 4:19). But remember, needs, not necessarily wants, will be provided.

As I mentioned previously, my budget has forty-two line items spread out over seven categories. When the Lord lays upon my heart to give a special offering, above what I have budgeted to give, I must obey! But how can I, when the line item for giving is empty? This is where the sacrifice comes in. I might go over to the clothing fund, and pull out an extra $100. If the Lord provided for Israel that their shoes and clothes did not wear out over forty years of wandering in the desert, then He can take care of my clothing needs (Deut. 29:5).

Or maybe I reach into the Christmas budget and pull out $200. If the Lord wants me to give this money, then either we won't have any needs at Christmas, He will replace those funds (or gifts), or my wife will find some really good deals. I don't know which it will be, and we may just go without new Christmas gifts. That is why it is a sacrifice. If the Lord lays upon my heart to give it away, then I must obey, for I am steward of His resources, not mine.

$200 is one thing, but what about when the Lord requests a special offering, and I must pull $5,000 out of my car fund? What do I do then? I have my purposes and goals for that car fund. I have a target date in which I will save enough funds to purchase the car. Yet if the Lord asks me to give His money away, I am His steward. He will take care of me. I can trust Him.

Wasted Giving

One of the most difficult aspects of giving is the feeling that the gift is wasted. Why should I give my hard-earned money when it is going to be wasted? There are two types of wasted giving I will address. The first is when I give incorrectly. The second is when my gift appears to have gone to the wrong cause. One is frustrating in the moment, the other is frustrating in the future.

1. The Wasted Attitude of Grouchiness

It has often been said, "God loves a cheerful giver, but He'll take it from a grouch." While this is true, the attitude of a grouch results in a wasted gift. God does not need your gift. You need to give your gift. It is a heart attitude. Do you have a covetous spirit? Or do you recognize your job is to be a steward of God's resources?

Remember the term we used from the Bible called a "heave offering"? That is the same word used in Proverbs 29:4, which speaks of a conquering king requiring tribute.

> *The king by judgment establisheth the land: but he that receiveth gifts overthroweth it. (Pr. 29:4)*

The Jews hated giving tribute to foreign kings. They did all that they could to eliminate their tax burdens. It is the same in our culture today. I do all that I legally can to lower my tax obligations (more on that later). Some people treat their giving the same way. It is a line item that they know they ought to give because God wants them to give, but they sure would give less if they could get away with it!

I had someone ask me before: Should I tithe on my gross income or my net income? Here is my response, "Do you want God to bless you on your gross income, or just your net income?" But the truth is, that mentality is just another way of saying, "I would give less if I could." That attitude turns your giving into a wasted gift. God does not need your offerings, but you need to give offerings to help cure your covetous heart!

> *Wherefore the Lord said, Forasmuch as this people draw near me with their mouth, and with their lips do honour me, but have removed their heart far from me, and their fear toward me is taught by the precept of men. (Is. 29:13)*

2. The Wasted Attitude of Pride

There are those who are trying to give more, but only if others may see them give. These are the types who seek to have buildings named in their honor. They want the whole world to know what they gave to a particular organization. They like to be called philanthropists. This comes from a heart of pride.

> *Take heed that ye do not your alms before men, to be*
> *seen of them: otherwise ye have no reward of your Father*
> *which is in heaven. Therefore when thou doest thine alms,*
> *do not sound a trumpet before thee, as the hypocrites*
> *do in the synagogues and in the streets, that they may*
> *have glory of men. Verily I say unto you, They have their*
> *reward. But when thou doest alms, let not thy left hand*
> *know what thy right hand doeth: That thine alms may*
> *be in secret: and thy Father which seeth in secret himself*
> *shall reward thee openly. (Mt. 6:1-4)*

There is, quite possibly, no worse sin in the eyes of God than pride. The only way a sinner can be born into the family of God is to admit (against his own pride) that he is an evil, nasty sinner incapable of saving himself. Pride is what keeps most sinners away from God's grace. But pride has also caused a lot of giving to go to waste.

When Jesus spoke of "sounding a trumpet," there is much debate as to whether this was an actual practice, a metaphor for the clanging of the money in the offering box, or a Jewish collo-quialism equivalent to "tooting your own horn." It has been suggested that some Pharisees may have brought their alms gifts in the form of small coins so that as it was dumped into the treasury, it created a louder and longer sound for all to hear.

Whichever interpretation is the truth of Jesus's words, the application is the same. These Pharisees were giving to be seen and heard of men. Christ condemned this type of giving and highlighted the importance of giving "in secret." No greater illustration is given than the story found in Acts 5 of Ananias and Sapphira. After seeing the praise heaped upon those who dedicated all they had to the Lord, they wanted in on the praise. So, in a deceitful manner, they sold their possession, and brought only a portion of the monies to give. They indicated that they were giving all the proceeds to the Lord. They lied, and the Lord's reprimand was severe.

> But Peter said, Ananias, why hath Satan filled thine heart to lie to the Holy Ghost, and to keep back part of the price of the land? Whiles it remained, was it not thine own? And after it was sold, was it not in thine own power? Why hast thou conceived this thing in thine heart? Thou hast not lied unto men, but unto God. And Ananias hearing these words fell down, and gave up the ghost: and great fear came on all them that heard these things. (Acts 5:3-5)

You may be able to trick those around you about what you give, but God knows the heart. Ananias and Sapphira lost their lives, and their reward from God for their gift, because it was given to receive the praise of men.

Recently, a man in our church was a little upset about something and asked, "Do you know how much I give?" I answered "No, we don't look at who gives what." Though his original giving may not have been done in pride (or maybe it was, I don't know), in that moment, Satan used it to turn his heart bitter. Pride had crept into his heart unawares. What was first given in love for the Lord then became a source of pride.

The Pharisees of the New Testament had a practice that appeared to be spiritual, but was nothing more than covetousness. This was a practice Jesus condemned in Mark 7. It was called "Corban." The Pharisees would often show their piety to God by declaring all their goods were "Corban," or a dedication to the temple treasury. As the stewards of God's treasures, they could of course live on their income, but they could not spend any money on the "frivolous" things. They considered supporting their own aging parents financially as frivolous. They deemed it a "sacrilege" to use God's money to support their elderly parents.

This practice showed the heart of the Pharisees was full of covetousness. They coveted the applause of men for their false piety, rather than seeking the applause of God by honoring their father and mother (Ex. 20:12). They wanted men to think highly of their generosity, while simultaneously living with a covetous sprit. That type of attitude is despicable to God, and it results in wasted giving.

3. The Wasted Recipient

Several years ago, it was revealed that a man from the church I attended during college had embezzled from the church multiple hundreds of thousands of dollars. The man did not work for the church, he was a part of the offering counting team. Somehow, he had worked out a way to steal cash from the church without being caught for almost seven years. It was not my money he stole, because I always wrote a check. Nevertheless, there was a twinge of sorrow even in my heart when the news broke.

I have often given money to someone only later to wonder if the recipient was genuine, or if my gift really made any difference. Periodically a story will come out of a panhandler who receives more in donations than I make working full time. Occasionally I will hear of a charity that spends 80 percent of their funds on advertisement to receive more funds. If I gave to such a cause, I always feel bad. There were so many other needs, how could I waste the money God gave me on that which was not genuine?

As a steward, the money is not mine, it belongs to the Lord, and I am the manager. It is my responsibility to use those funds wisely in my own budget, as well as what is given away. But sometimes, the Lord will lay on your heart to give to a cause which later you discover was unworthy to receive the donation. What then?

You cannot always control what the recipient will do with the money God directs you to give on His behalf. But that is okay, you don't have to. Unless God has made you an overseer of that ministry, it is no longer your responsibility. You did your part, let God do His. It was not your money anyway, it belonged to God. Despite hundreds of thousands of dollars embezzled, that church I attended was still the strongest (financially) church I had ever seen. God took the leftover, and multiplied it to do His work, despite the evil practiced by a church member.

Truly the only wasted gift is one where the heart of the giver is not right. If you have sought the Lord's direction, give from a right heart and a joyful spirit. God can take even a wasted gift and make it something good.

CHAPTER 4

Investing That Pleases God

ᐯᏜ

As a steward of God's money, I must seek His direction for distributing to His causes. I also must seek His direction for spending upon myself. But there is a third principle that is vitally important, and is the topic of thousands of books. How do I invest my money for the future?

Should A Christian Invest?

Back in the 1970s, there was a sweeping movement among Bible-believing churches that retirement investing was wasting God's money. Christ would be soon returning, so let's use His money to spread the gospel today. While the sentiment may be good, it was actually an unbiblical philosophy. God requires His stewards to prepare (financially) for their future.

A good man leaveth an inheritance to his children's children: and the wealth of the sinner is laid up for the just. (Pr. 13:22)

There is treasure to be desired and oil in the dwelling of the wise; but the foolish man spendeth it up. (Pr. 21:20)

> *The thoughts of the diligent tend only to plenteousness; but*
> *of every one that is hasty only to want. (Pr. 21:5)*

Investing is a tricky matter for a Christian. If God owns the cattle on a thousand hills, and the wealth in every mine (Ps. 50:10, Hag. 2:8), why should I prepare for the future? God can just take care of me then. While it is true that God can take care of you, and that He will take care of His servants, He also commands His servants to save. And not just save a little, but as Proverbs 13:22 says, save enough to leave an inheritance to your grandchildren. That is multigenerational wealth.

In the parable of the unjust steward, the Lord commended the unjust steward for his wisdom. Even though he had squandered the stewardship, he had prepared for himself beyond his appointed stewardship (Lk. 16:8). Then Jesus made a very unusual statement.

> *And I say unto you, Make to yourselves friends of the*
> *mammon of unrighteousness; that, when ye fail, they may*
> *receive you into everlasting habitations. He that is faithful*
> *in that which is least is faithful also in much: and he that*
> *is unjust in the least is unjust also in much. If therefore ye*
> *have not been faithful in the unrighteous mammon, who*
> *will commit to your trust the true riches? (Lk. 16:9-11)*

I would be deceiving you if I said that I fully understood the application of this parable, but there are a few key points. First, Christ wants us to make friends of the "mammon of unrigh-teousness." This is literally saying to have rich friends who do not follow God. There may be a few reasons for this. One might be to share the love of Christ with that individual, but another is to learn wealth management so that you might be "faithful in that which is least."

The "true riches" are the things concerning the Kingdom of God. The knowledge of God, your relationship with God, and the sharing of that knowledge with others that they might also know God. Christ indicates that if you are unable to handle the lesser things (like wealth), why should you be entrusted to handle the more valuable things (like the knowledge of God)? Christ therefore places emphasis on understanding wealth management.

Christ quickly follows up the parable with the reminder in verse 13 that "No servant can serve two masters... ye cannot serve God and mammon." We are to understand wealth, but not serve wealth. We are still stewards of God's wealth, not our own. So what are some things we can learn from the Bible and from the world that will help us become better wealth managers?

Usury

Usury is the Bible term for interest. If you pay 4 percent interest on a home mortgage or a car loan, you are paying usury. If you pay 25 percent interest on a credit card loan, you are paying usury. If you have lent out your own money with the expectation of receiving interest (such as a bond), then you are expecting usury. The Bible actually has a lot to say about usury, some things good, and some things bad. Not everything the Bible says about usury conforms to the thinking of our world, so we will look at both, and then determine how to invest for usury.

If thou lend money to any of my people that is poor by thee, thou shalt not be to him as a usurer, neither shalt thou lay upon him usury. (Ex. 22:25)

And if thy brother be waxen poor, and fallen in decay with thee; then thou shalt relieve him: yea, though he be a stranger, or a sojourner; the he may live with thee. Take thou no usury of him, or increase: but fear thy God; that thy brother may live with thee. Thou shalt not give him thy money upon usury, nor lend him thy victuals for increase. (Lev. 25:35-37)

There are definite circumstances in which God forbade His people from lending on usury. If a brother (or a stranger living among Israel) was poor, they were forbidden from lending with the expectation of interest paid. They were allowed to lend, but should only expect the return to equal the amount lent.

This is completely backwards from our society today! Those who are poorest receive the highest interest rates, because they are the greatest risk.[6] The highest interest rates in America are not from credit cards, they are Payday loan lenders. Payday lenders target poor communities and those on social security, and they charge the highest usury of any lending program. If you were to invest in a biblical manner, you ought to avoid being a part of such a group!

Referring back to the previous chapter on tithing and giving, the Church is not bound to the same laws that Israel was bound to keep. The Church is under grace. So why should a Christian adhere to this type of restriction? If it is one of the most profitable loan types, then it would be financially beneficial to be a lender in this way. Would that not be learning from the unrighteous mammon of which Christ spoke?

The purpose of the law was to reveal the differences between the character of God, and the wickedness of man. The character of God reveals that He watches over the poor. Those who are poor through no means of their own wastefulness (more about that later) have a special place in God's heart. He watches over them. He blesses those who will bless them, and He curses those who will curse them.

> *He that hath pity upon the poor lendeth unto the LORD; and that which he hath given will he pay him again. (Pr. 19:17)*

> *He that oppresseth the poor to increase his riches, and he that giveth to the rich, shall surely come to want. (Pr. 22:16)*

God also forbade His people from lending upon usury to their brethren.

> *Thou shalt not lend upon usury to thy brother; usury of money, usury of victuals, usury of any thing that is lent upon usury: Unto a stranger thou mayest lend upon usury; but unto thy brother thou shalt not lend upon usury... (Deut. 23:19-20)*

God designed this law so that the Israelites would not have the social inequality present in other countries. If a brother needed money, an Israelite was to lend with no expectation of interest.

To a stranger (or a non-Israelite), they were allowed to lend with usury (unless the recipient was poor).

The Church is not the same as Israel, but if this principle was to be applied, a Christian ought never to lend money to a brother (familially or spiritually) who has need with the expectation of an interest return. This would not apply to lending to a stranger, or a neighbor, or a bank with the intent of gaining interest, so long as that institution is not using those funds to oppress the poor.

Acceptable Financial Returns

You might ask then, "How can I invest if I cannot lend to a brother or to the poor?" In Christ's parable of the talents, there were mentioned two investment categories that would be acceptable. I believe there are also others that could fit within biblical principles.

> Then he that had received the five talents went and traded with the same, and made them other five talents. (Mt. 25:16)

> Thou oughtest therefore to have put my money to the exchangers, and then at my coming I should have received mine own with usury. (Mt. 25:27)

Here Christ gives a distinction between high-risk and low-risk investments. The high-risk, and high work investment was a business venture or trading of goods (purchasing something low and selling it for a profit). It was purchasing something at wholesale and selling it at retail. This was not a "get rich quick scheme"; it was a business model of hard work. It was hustle. This investment involved speculation and risk due to the unknown variables of customer demand. It was an active investment that provided the necessary living for the servant as well as a 100 percent gain for the master.

The first two stewards worked actively to grow an investment to a greater return. The third steward was a sluggard. But the Master identifies an investment type for the sluggard too. There was an investment that was passive so that the lazy man did not need to do anything. It did not have as great a return, but it would have been more acceptable than burying the money. The low-risk, low-reward investment was to give the money to the bank, so that they might profit for the master. Then he would have received a small portion of their profits as a reward for lending them the talent.

America has dozens, and probably hundreds of different investment vehicles. Some are active, and some are passive. Either one is acceptable, so long as they do not conflict with other Bible principles. It is okay to take a low-risk approach and let someone else grow your money. It will yield a low return. It is also okay to actively manage your wealth for a higher return. From this passage, and many others, here are a few examples of acceptable and unacceptable styles of investing:

Acceptable- Active Business Ventures involving hard work and speculative returns (starting an online marketplace, a consulting firm, etc., or purchasing and running a restaurant, a hair salon etc.).

Unacceptable- Active Business Ventures that violate the Holy Spirit's leading and the character of God (such as businesses promoting ungodliness; strip clubs, bars, pornographic websites, etc.).

Acceptable- Passive Business Ventures involving someone else's hard work and risk (such as purchasing a company or piece of a company for a share of the profits). The most common form of this style investing is purchasing shares of companies with the expectation of receiving a dividend (more about this later).

Unacceptable- Passive Business Ventures that abuse one of God's principles (such as owning shares in a tobacco company, as addressed in Chapter 1).

Acceptable- Active Interest Investing to businesses and the wealthy (such as "hard money lending" to fund construction of a house for a business to sell at profit).

Unacceptable- Active Interest Investing to the downtrodden (such as high interest loans to those who cannot afford the interest). This was a very common practice of banks in 2007-2008, who would offer loan programs to "help" poor people buy homes they could not afford. They included negative amortized loans with balloon payments, "NINJA" loans, and "ARM" loans. These put people who were already struggling into worse financial situations under the guise of helping the poor.

Acceptable- Passive Interest Investing in corporate lending ventures (such as bank savings, credit unions, corporate or municipal bonds)

Unacceptable- Passive Interest Investing to "shark lenders" (such as payday loans, debt collector agencies, and possibly credit card asset-backed securities)

The Necessity of Long-Term Thinking

Before the industrial revolution, it was necessary for individuals to plan out and ration their food for months at a time. Having an abundance in October was necessary to last through the harsh winter. There are many historical examples of failure to plan. The Jamestown colonists of 1609 were totally unprepared for the food shortages through the winter, and were unable to leave the fort without risking death by the native Powhatan Indians.[7] In the spring of 1610, only sixty of the original 300 colonists were still alive. Thousands of other examples could be given where people did not accurately plan for the future.

In Bible times, God designed a method of care for a person once he or she was too old to care for themselves. It was called children. But God wanted the worker to provide financially so that they could be cared for without being a burden financially (2 Cor. 12:14; Pr. 13:22). That required long-term planning. How can we make sure that our resources outlive us?

In America, and most other first world countries, the responsibility of caring for the elderly has shifted. People now believe the government should care for the elderly. It is the common economic theory of younger adults that the government will provide the "Social Security" needed for retirement. This is a destructive mindset (more on this later). God did not institute government to care for the aged. God did not institute government to provide for the poor. God's design was that workers would plan ahead for themselves, and that the people's generosity would provide for the downtrodden (alms giving). So how can we think long term?

1. Think First About Your Purpose

Purpose has already been discussed at length, but it is often overlooked when planning for retirement. For many, retirement is when they live for themselves, not for God. There is nothing wrong with enjoying your retirement, but retirement ought to be merely a transition from the world's employment to God's employment.

A similar parallel is brought up by Paul in 1 Corinthians 7 concerning marriage. Before a lady is married, she can dedicate herself to serving the Lord. After she is married, her time is split between serving the Lord and serving her husband. If you are employed (or even if you are the employer), you have the cares of this world that require your attention. You must balance your service toward God with your service toward your employer. Upon retirement (or partial retirement), you ought to have more time to serve God.

Increased service toward God will only become a reality if it is your purpose. If your purpose is travel, then travel you will. If your purpose is sports, then you will have a sporting good time indulging in athletics. If your purpose is God, then you will occupy your time with the things of God.

I serve as a chaplain in several retirement homes. They can be the most depressing places you've ever seen. Seniors who cannot care for themselves are often left to sit in front of a TV from breakfast until lunch, then from lunch until dinner, and then from dinner until bed. They have no purpose, and they waste away until death. But there are others who use their retirement to serve God. Some have started daily Bible studies with their friends. Some listen constantly to preachers on TV.

There was a lady I ministered to whose name was Ina. She was ninety-eight years old when she passed away. Every time I went into her room to visit, she had a large print Bible on her lap. Sometimes she was reading it, sometimes she was staring off into space, meditating upon what she had read. For two years, every single time I entered her room she was either in bed asleep, or in her chair with the Bible upon her lap. She was the only lady I've ever known who was a born again Christian for over ninety years. But Christianity was not just something she did, it was her purpose. She lived to know God and serve Him.

2. Think About Financially Providing For That Purpose

If your purpose is going to be to travel the world assisting missionaries (as mine is), then you need to consider what it will take to provide financially for that purpose. Will $100,000 annually be sufficient to fulfill that purpose? Will it only require $50,000 annually? Is your purpose to contribute large financial gifts to the cause of Christ? Will you need $500,000 annually to accomplish that purpose? Or is your purpose to stay close to home and serve in your local church as a volunteer secretary and receptionist? Will you need $30,000 annually to accomplish that purpose? Will $20,000 be sufficient?

Once you know your purpose, and you establish a baseline amount, then you can plan out how to achieve that purpose. If you want to retire at seventy years old, and expect to live until eighty years old fulfilling your purpose, then your retirement nest egg will need to be significantly smaller than if you want to retire at fifty and expect to live until 100 years old, fulfilling your purpose.

The common statement among financial advisors is that "Retirement is not an age, it is a number." What is the number you need to retire? To determine this number, many advisors use the 4 percent rule (you can choose 3 percent or less if you'd like). The 4 percent rule shows that if your retirement nest egg had been invested 50 percent into the stock market broadly and 50 percent into the bond market broadly, and you withdrew 4 percent of those funds annually (increasing annually according to inflation) that there would never have been a thirty-year period (in the markets) where your funds would have run out, therefore it is assumed that a 4 percent withdrawal rate is a safe rate to live in retirement for thirty years.[8]

If you choose to be more risky and diversify into different asset classes, you may be able to secure a higher withdrawal rate. If you are more risk averse and choose a less risky diversification, then a lower withdrawal rate would be necessary to meet the same requirements.

Applying the 4 percent rule to our hypothetical purpose of traveling the world assisting missionaries for 30 years at $100,000 annual needed withdrawal rate, then your original nest egg would need to be $2.5 million diversified 50/50 in stocks and bonds to ensure you could satisfy that purpose. To many, this seems like an unobtainable number. That is why thinking financially long-term, and diligent Bible-based investing is required (strategies will be discussed later).

3. Think About Your Legacy

Beyond simply investing to fulfill your God-given purpose, you also need to consider leaving an inheritance or legacy gifts upon your passing. I am still young, and many years away from my retirement purpose, but even today my wife and I have outlined what would happen with our resources should we unexpectedly pass away. It is simply good stewardship of God's resources to plan in this fashion.

Your first responsibility is to care for your spouse in the event you pass away before they do. You may live to be eighty years old, but your spouse may live to be 100. How will they be provided for in such a case? Your second responsibility is to make sure you leave a love gift to your children or grandchildren.

An inheritance left to children or grandchildren needs to have some strings attached. First, do not let your children know your financial abundance, unless they can be trusted. More families have been destroyed from jealousies and hurts surrounding an inheritance than can be counted. The spirit of covetousness often rears its ugly head when the will is involved.

You may also choose to leave out some or all of your children or grandchildren from the will. This should not be done inequitably, but it could be that a child has proven themselves to be lazy and wasteful, or even addicted to drugs. You must not fund their addiction. In these cases, it is best to leave in a written will or trust the requirements necessary for obtaining the inheritance.

It is common for grandparents to leave their grandchildren an inheritance with the stipulation that they cannot access the funds except for a house or college. Just remember, all such stipulations need to be fair, and in legally binding documents.

If you have diligently trained up your children in sound biblical principles, they may not need an inheritance. You may still choose to leave funds for them, but maybe you have excess amounts that can be left as a legacy gift to your church, or other charitable organization. What a difference a $2 million trust fund to support missionaries in Brazil could make in spreading the gospel.

In 1938, Mr. William Herman Bolthouse took over the family farm from his parents. He was a Christian man who had a special desire to further missions work in Brazil. In 2005 he sold a majority stake in his company, "Bolthouse Farms," to Madison Dearborn Partners for an astounding $1.12 billion valuation. With those funds, Mr. Bolthouse founded the Bolthouse Foundation. In 2018, the Bolthouse Foundation contributed $18 million to charitable organizations, including much of that to missionaries in Brazil.[9]

A legacy gift can further your purpose even after you pass away. Just make sure any legacy gifts have the proper oversight to ensure they are accessed and spent according to your wishes.

King David left what was probably the most significant legacy gift the world has ever known. It was one of David's greatest desires to build a temple for God. God became his purpose. Everything he did in his older years was aimed toward that purpose, building the temple. God denied him this desire, stating he had shed too much blood (God did not want His temple associated with bloodshed). Instead, God promised that David's son would have the honor of building the temple. David did not get mad and pout, instead, he began to diligently prepare for that eventuality. He left a legacy gift.

Now I have prepared with all my might for the house of my God the gold for things to be made of gold, and the silver for things of silver, and the brass for things of brass, the iron for things of iron, and wood for things of wood; onyx stones, and stones to be set, glistering stones, and of diverse colours, and all manner of precious stones, and marble stones in abundance. Moreover, because I have set my affection to the house of my God, I have of mine own proper good, of gold and silver, which I have given to the house of my God, over and above all that I have prepared for the holy house, Even three thousand talents of gold, and the silver for things of silver, and for all manner of work to be made by the hands of artificers. And who then is willing to consecrate his service this day unto the LORD? (1 Chron. 29:2-5)

After 3,000 years we still call that first temple "Solomon's Temple," but it was made possible by the legacy gift of Solomon's father, King David. What legacy gift might you leave that would impact eternity? Don't allow your children or grandchildren to squander the stewardship God has given to you. Leave your stewardship to a faithful steward (Lk. 12:42).

The Folly of Wealth Accumulation

As has been previously stated, wealth accumulation is not a biblical or Christ-honoring purpose. Wealth is a tool to fulfill God's purposes. There is no need to continue to accumulate wealth just for the sake of accumulating wealth. "He who dies with the most toys still dies." You cannot take your wealth with you into eternity, but you can receive reward in the next life for what type of steward you are in this life (Mt. 25:23).

Have you ever thought of this: Every richest man in the world up until the 1900s has died, and every richest man in the world still alive today will one day die. At the time of this writing the wealthiest and greatest investor of all time is undoubtedly Warren Buffet. He is the CEO of Berkshire Hathaway. He has personally accumulated nearly $90 billion in wealth and is at the time of this writing the fourth wealthiest man in the world. He is also now in his nineties. He will die one day, and the "Oracle of Omaha" (as he is often called) will take none of it with him.

In the late 1800s and early 1900s, John D. Rockefeller was a tycoon of industry owning 90 percent of the U.S. oil and gas industry, as well as much of the railroad industry.[10] His personal net worth was about 1 percent of the entire U.S. economy. When asked, "How much money is enough?" he is said to have responded, "Just a little bit more." He passed away in 1937, and he took none of his wealth with him. There is much good that can be done with wealth, but only if it is used. Simply accumulating wealth is pointless, and has no lasting value to you.

Jesus gave the story of a rich fool. Look at what He said:

And he spake a parable unto them, saying, The ground of a certain rich man brought forth plentifully: and he thought within himself, saying, What shall I do, because I have no room where to bestow my fruits? And he said, This will I do: I will pull down my barns, and build greater; and there will I bestow all my fruits and my goods. And I will say to my soul, Soul, thou hast much goods laid up for many years; take thine ease, eat, drink, and be merry. But God said unto him, Thou fool, this night thy soul shall be required of thee: then whose shall those things be, which thou hast provided? So is he that layeth up treasure for himself, and is not rich toward God. (Lk. 12:16-21)

When wealth accumulation is the end, not the means to an end, then God declares "thou fool." Many might argue that this rich man was wise. He discovered the secrets of good business. He was planning for the future. He was diligently preparing in faith for a greater harvest to come. But he was laying up treasure for himself and was not rich toward God. Wealth accumulation is folly. It is a terrible purpose. Money is simply a tool that can be used for God, or for self. It should be used for God.

Biblically Sound Investment Strategies

There are many Bible principles to help determine how to invest for the short term (such as purchasing a car) or for long term (such as retirement). As previously discussed, there are acceptable and unacceptable forms of investment. We must always ask, "Would God be pleased with this investment?" Let's examine some biblical strategies to answer these questions.

1. <u>Managing Risk</u>

There is no such thing as a risk-free investment. No matter how carefully you invest, and no matter how safe the investments appear to be, there is still risk. Every investor needs to determine how much risk they are willing to take with the stewardship God has provided.

In my short investing career, I have taken some major risks. I had money I did not immediately need, which I determined to invest into some short-term, high-risk investments. Some did very well, others did very poorly. After one incredibly great six-week performance, I reinvested funds into another investment, and lost 95 percent over the course of three weeks. It was quite painful to see my gains dwindle into losses. What I learned from that experience was this concept of managing risk. Higher risk often has the potential for extreme returns, but it also has the potential for extreme losses.

Once I know my purpose, and have my goal set, I can begin contributing into a long-term investment vehicle such as an IRA, pension plan, syndicate, or a brokerage account. From there, I can determine my risk tolerance, and ways to manage risk.

Recently I met with my financial advisor and IRA custodian for an annual check-up to outline goals and strategies for the upcoming year. I am a "low value" client, because I have less than $100,000 in that brokerage account. I have a long-time horizon with that account (retirement), and I accept moderate to high risk in that account (100 percent stocks invested in four major groupings). There really is not a lot to discuss. We talked about asset allocation, and continued contribution amounts. It was just a check-up.

But when a client crosses fifty years of age, things start to pick up in these types of management situations. As a client approaches retirement, the custodian will begin to divest from high-risk industries and assets into lower risk (such as bonds). There is a fine line to balance between asset appreciation and asset preservation. The last thing you want is to see a 95 percent drop in your portfolio the year before you intend to retire.

a.   Diversify Your Portfolio

Amazingly, the Bible actually talks about diversifying investments.

> *Cast thy bread upon the waters: for thou shalt find it after many days. Give a portion to seven, and also to eight; for thou knowest not what evil shall be upon the earth. (Ecc. 11:1-2)*

Solomon equates "bread" with wealth. "Casting the bread upon the waters" is used to describe investing your wealth. It leaves your possession for a time so that it can come back to you when you need it. Verse 2 talks about giving a portion to seven or to eight. This is essentially the same as saying, "Don't put all your eggs in one basket." If you are going to invest, don't go all in on one stock. Diversify.

Back to my hard-learned lesson on diversification. I had seen a dip in Microsoft stock (MSFT), and had assumed that it was a short-term blip. I then invested several thousand dollars into call options expiring in two months. Over the following few days, the stock continued to drop. I chose to sell my other positions and go all in on the same options position I had taken (dollar cost averaging down). After three weeks, my $40,000 portfolio had a book value of only $2,000. It was a difficult decision to sell those options at such a steep loss, but it was the right decision. By the time those options expired, they expired worthless.

My basket was not large enough. I piled into a single position, and lost 95 percent of my portfolio in only a few short weeks. One way to manage risk is to diversify. Fortunately, this was not my only investment vehicle. This was only a short-term investment account for a specific upcoming project. Had this been my entire wealth, I'd have set myself back many years over one foolish investment decision.

b.   Diversify Your Asset Types

There are a few very common investment sectors. The Technology Sector was a very well performing sector in 2020. It was also a very high-performance asset class in 1999. If you were in the markets in 1999, you will remember that any company with a "dot com" at the end of its name was on an upward trajectory, and appeared to only have growth on the horizon. Then came the crash. On March 10, 2000 the NASDAQ index peaked at $5,048.62; on October 4, 2002 it crested at $1,139.90. A 77 percent decrease in thirty-one months.

But not all sectors sustained such gargantuan loses. In fact, real estate in the U.S. increased over those same thirty-one months by an average of 16 percent (according to DQYDJ Historical

Median Home Prices).[11] Sometimes, asset class performance is inversely correlated with another asset class (such as the commodities market, typically inversely correlated to USD). Exposure to multiple asset classes will help mitigate risk.

When the Covid-19 pandemic popped up its ugly head, almost overnight all asset classes crashed. But they did not all stay in the dumps. Immediately, particular asset groups begin to rally, while others stayed in a bear market. The travel industry stocks plummeted and stayed low, because very few people were travelling. But particular tech stocks soared to new all-time highs as people moved to a more digital work and school environment. In my personal portfolio, I made a significant gain on some of my positions, while others sustained a significant loss. Overall, I made money through the pandemic because I was diversified into different sectors.

2. Stock and Bond Investing

Stock investing can be fun. It is super exciting for a new investor to see that first ten cent deposit into their brokerage account from a dividend paying company. That ten cents represents a way to increase your portfolio and get you to that future goal just a little bit sooner. It is also exciting to see the value increase from your stock positions (asset appreciation). But is stock investing ethical?

A stock is ownership. Some businesses have chosen to sell their companies to millions (or billions) of little owners. So being a shareholder makes you the "master" in the story of the talents. As a "master," you are entitled to the profits earned from the "stewards" who run the company.

So, stock appreciation and dividend growth are ethical methods of growing wealth if the business you own is an ethical business. Chapter 1 examined the need to ethically choose which companies are worthy of investment. This is why it is vital that you select your investments in accordance with what would please your Master (Jesus Christ). Would Jesus find a beer company an acceptable place to invest? If not, then neither should a Christian. Purchasing shares of a company is purchasing that company.

> *Be ye not unequally yoked together with unbelievers: for what fellowship hath righteousness with unrighteousness? And that communion hath light with darkness? And what concord hath Christ with Belial? Or what part hath he that believeth with an infidel? (2 Cor. 6:14)*

What about bonds? A bond is debt. We've already discussed the stipulations that the Israelites had for lending upon usury. Should a Christian be involved in the bond market? If a Christian wishes to follow the standards God placed upon the Israelites, then he must be sure that the bonds purchased fit the Old Testament standard. Ethical companies who are able to repay their debts are acceptable under the Old Testament standards.

3. Leveraged Investing (Debt)

Leveraged investing is debt upon an investment. Most Americans at some point will have leveraged investing, even if they did not recognize what it was. Leverage is using funds available as collateral to borrow more funds. The most common form of leveraged investing is when someone purchases a home using a mortgage. The down payment (sometimes as low as 3.5 percent) is leveraged to borrow the remaining purchase price of a home, and the home's ownership note is held as collateral against repayment of the mortgage debt. Is it ethical to leverage your money? Is it ethical to acquire debt?

The rich ruleth over the poor, and the borrower is servant to the lender. (Pr. 22:7)

As long as someone has debt, they are subservient in some way to the lender of that debt. There are, however, a few different types of debt. There are collateralized debts (asset backed debt), and there are non-collateralized debts (or non-asset backed). The functionality of these debts has a lot to do with the moral implications of debt.

a. Non Collateralized Debt Obligations

The most common forms of non-collateralized debts are credit card debts, student loans, and medical bills. These debts are guaranteed to the lender upon the word of the borrower. The borrower becomes a slave to that debt (as Proverbs 22:7 describes). If the debt is neglected or defaults (not paid), the lender has no recourse against the purchased item. Instead, their recourse is against the borrower directly because the borrower gave their word that the debt would be repaid. This means that the debt is collateralized against the word of the borrower.

b. Collateralized Debt Obligations

Collateralized debt is debt held on an item, not an individual. If I cannot fulfil my obligation to pay the loan on my house, the bank repossesses the asset (the house), and sells it to fulfill the obligations. The bank will not repossess my car to pay off my house, nor will they repossess my house to pay off my car. There is a limit to what can be collected as payment for my obligation.

Incorporation is a common way to collateralize debt. If debts are unable to be repaid, the business is sued and dissolved to repay the lenders, but the lender cannot sue the owner without a just (legal) cause to "pierce the corporate veil" (such as fraud).

c. Using Leverage

In the business world, using leverage (debt) is common, and in many instances necessary. But in the personal realm, most investors are scared to use leverage. That is because leverage constitutes risk. A company generating $10 million in annual revenue may feel that an infusion of $100 million of debt will allow them to scale up and achieve $50 million in annual revenue. It is thereby deemed a "good use" of risk. Things may not work out as they hoped, but the high reward justified the risk of taking on substantial leverage. But in the personal realm, that risk is just too high.

When my wife and I purchased our first home (a condo), we paid 5 percent of the purchase price as a down payment, and borrowed the remaining 95 percent. It was the only way we could afford a condo in our area. After much prayer and consideration, the numbers just made good sense. Our monthly costs to own the condo were less than the monthly costs to rent an apartment. The leverage became a helpful tool, and outweighed the risk of that debt. We did a similar thing (though with a greater down payment) when we later purchased our house.

Many well-known financial advisors advise against this type of borrowing. Surely it would be better to have paid cash for the condo, and for the house, but that was not an option. If we had attempted to save up a larger down payment, it would have taken several more years of saving and investing, and the price appreciation of the home we purchased would have outstripped the pace at which we could save.

Leverage can be a tool in investing as well, but it also increases risk. For a while, I had used my stock portfolio to borrow more money to invest. A $5,000 portfolio then had the ability to hold $7,500 in stocks at my brokerage. During a bull market (a time when asset prices are consistently increasing), I profited greatly from that extra $2,500, and it quickly was paid back from the sale of some appreciated positions. But then one day, I received a margin call.

A margin call is when the balance of the portfolio held at the brokerage falls below their minimum "safety buffer." I was given three days to deposit additional funds or sell off some positions. I did not want to sell the positions I had, because they had lost value, and I believed they would return to higher values, so I deposited some extra funds to supply the difference needed. Because the account was relatively small (below $10,000) the margin call was easily addressable. Had I received a margin call on a substantially larger position, I would have been unable to cover the needed deposits, and I would have been forced to sell some positions at a loss.

Introducing leverage into an investment creates greater potential for positive returns, but also introduces increased risk for negative returns. When seeking how to fulfill your purpose with investing and leverage, you must calculate the possibility of loss, your ability to cover that loss, and then determine if it is worth the risk!

Speculative Investing and Gambling

The majority of Christians have heard, and many believe, that gambling is bad. Many, however, do not have a biblical understanding of why gambling may be bad, or how gambling is different than investing.

1. Gambling As Poor Stewardship?

The most common reason Christians often give for why gambling is bad is that it is poor stewardship of God's money. I fully agree that if you lose, it is poor stewardship, but what if you win? How can a win really be called poor stewardship? There must be a deeper reason why gambling is wrong, or else it could very easily be argued that it is no different than investing.

Others have said that gambling is entertainment. And it certainly can be entertaining for a time! Years ago, I pastored a small chapel in a resort town near a casino. One of the members of the church would often go to the casino, purchase lunch, and then set a budget to gamble $20 on the slot machines. This was an older, single man in his mid-eighties, a man who had been a Christian longer than I had been alive. I really did not have a biblical reason (at the time) to rebuke him for his gambling habit.

Many people in the town owned boats and wave runners (as he did). Owning a wave runner was a lot more expensive than a

$20 weekly trip to the casino, and sometimes he even returned with a profit. How was his "entertainment" any different than blowing hundreds of dollars on gas for speed boats, or purchasing tickets to a Lakers basketball game? While most who struggle with gambling do face a stewardship issue, I believe there is a stronger reason why the Holy Spirit leads Christians to avoid gambling.

Thou shalt not defraud thy neighbor, neither rob him: the wages of him that is hired shall not abide with thee all night unto the morning. (Lev. 19:13)

Here then is an obscure rule in a list of laws for the Jews. Christians are not bound to the Old Testament Law, as has been previously discussed, but God is still the same, and there is a principle here that is very applicable to this topic of gambling. Gambling defrauds your neighbor.

The word "defraud" means "to make destitute." In the context of Leviticus 19, there is a whole list of ways that someone might defraud their neighbor. Farmers were commanded by God to leave some of their fruits for the poor to glean, so over-harvesting the crop was defrauding the poor (more on that later). Stealing defrauded the neighbor. Lying defrauded the neighbor. Withholding earned pay was defrauding the neighbor. Cursing the deaf because they could not hear, or placing a stumbling block before the blind because they could not see, were both defrauding the neighbor. An unrighteous judge defrauds his neighbor. A talebearer (gossip), a false witness in court, hating thy brother, withholding needed rebuke, and taking revenge were all defrauding the neighbor (all listed in Leviticus 19).

I believe that in most circumstances, gambling is also defrauding your neighbor. When gambling, the only way I win is if someone else loses. The Holy Spirit of God will lead every Christian in the correct path, and we must heed that path. For me, the Holy Spirit has plainly shown me that if I win money by someone else losing (even if they know they might be losing) then I am defrauding my neighbor.

There is another reason the Holy Spirit has led me to believe that gambling is wrong. Gambling gets its appeal from the spirit of covetousness. This has already been discussed at length. As I listen to sports talk radio, the hosts often refer to the betting line. Often the statement will be made that the game is more fun when there is something on the line. What they are saying is that when your spirit of covetousness is being excited, the game is more exciting.

Recently, I was speaking with a Christian lady of over eighty years, at a retirement home. She commented to me that she had made a big mistake. She had received a flyer in the mail for the Publisher's Clearing House Sweepstakes. Excitedly, she responded, and purchased something from their catalog. For a day or two she dreamt of what it would be like to win the grand prize of $7,000 per week for life. Then the Lord smote her heart about her covetousness. The Lord had already taken care of all her needs, and yet she was greedy for more. This is what gambling does in the heart!

2. <u>Is Investing Gambling?</u>

Sometimes, investing can look like gambling. In fact, there are certain types of investing that are nothing more than a gamble.

How shall we avoid the gambler's mentality in our investing for the long term and for God's purpose? Remembering the two reasons the Holy Spirit has shown me concerning gambling (defrauding our neighbors and having a heart of covetousness), here are some practical tips for investing to ensure that it is not gambling.

a.   Dividend Investing Is Not Gambling.

A dividend is paid when the company does well. In essence, we all win together. A product or service is being provided by the company to the consumer, so the consumer wins. The consumer is paying a fair and acceptable price for the product or service to the company, so the company wins. The company is paying out a portion of those profits to their owners (the shareholders), so the shareholder wins. There is no defrauding going on in this scenario. And as long as your heart is not consumed with a spirit of covetousness, then you are investing, not gambling.

b.   Growth Stock Investing Is Not Gambling.

Some companies do not pay dividends. Is it gambling to invest in that company? Not usually. The company chooses to not pay out a dividend because either they need that money to continue their operations, or they feel they can scale up their business better with those funds. They are reinvesting profits back into themselves. In this case, your profit for investing in a company is based upon selling your ownership stake (your shares) for a higher price than the purchased price. Is it not a gamble that the price will go up? And is that defrauding my neighbor? If I choose to purchase a share of a company like Johnson and Johnson (JNJ) for $130 per share, and I hope to sell those shares down the road for $200 per share, how is that fair to my neighbor?

Selling shares at a profit is not defrauding your neighbor, because the company is more valuable (in the eyes of the purchaser) than it used to be. This week as I penned this chapter, I sold JNJ stock at $150 per share. I did not sell them because I felt the company was no longer worth that price, I sold because I wanted to take my gains and deploy that capital in a new location. Whoever purchased the shares from me (on the brokerage account) felt that the company was worth $150 per share. Therefore, no one was defrauded.

What if those shares drop from $150 back down to $100? Would not the person who purchased my shares have lost money? Yes, but nothing was done unethically (unless I had inside information). It was just bad timing.

c.   Speculative Investing Is Not Gambling.

There are also speculative investments. Is it gambling to purchase a stock (or company) on a speculative guess? Not always. Last year I purchased a single share of Tesla (TSLA) stock. I purchased at a far overvalued price compared to its peers. At the time, Tesla was only producing 130,000k vehicles per quarter, and was losing money. I had even sold some of my Ford (F) shares to purchase the Tesla share. It was a speculative investment. I believed (at the time) that the company's growth would cause the company to one day soon be worth more than I paid. I sold my share only a few weeks later for a massive profit. At the time of sale, I believed that the company was several years away from being intrinsically valued at the price the shares were trading.

Since I sold out, the share price has tripled in value again! As I study the financials and growth prospects of the company, I believe the company is over five years away from being intrinsically worth the share price today (Intrinsic value is the true value of all expected profits with a reasonable multiple applied). Even though I speculate that the company may even climb higher in share price, I don't believe the intrinsic value will meet my short-term time horizon, so I will not invest. Purchasing the company at the current price would be (to me) a gamble; a hope that someone else will gamble more than me and purchase at a higher price (the bigger fool mentality).

As of right now, I have many speculative investments in my trading accounts. I must be careful that I do not invest based upon a spirit of covetousness, but with a sound mind and purpose of glorifying God! If a particular investment increases in price beyond my time/price analysis and expectation, I will sell. I do not want to knowingly sell an ownership position (stock) in a company I believe will fail.

d.   Short Selling Is Gambling.

There is a particular investment strategy called a "short sale." I do not short sell the market. It is my belief that a short sell falls into the gambling category of defrauding my neighbor. You may not come to this conclusion, but I have, and here is why.

A short sale is a bet (or gamble) that everyone else will lose money. The short seller makes money when the investors lose value, and when the company loses money. This appears to me to be no different than gambling at the horse track. A short sale is borrowing someone's shares to sell with the promise of returning those shares at a later date.

A short sale is also uncollateralized debt. Because it is so risky, most brokerages require the cash from the sale to remain in the account until the debt has been satisfied. The idea is, someone borrows 100 shares to sell at today's price, places the proceeds into the brokerage account and waits for bad news. Once bad news has struck, the company stock price decreases, and the short seller repurchases the 100 shares at a lower price to return to the original borrower. The short seller profits from the difference. Basically, I win because you lose. This is defrauding your neighbor.

After writing this chapter's rough draft, a very unusual event happened in the stock market. It was a short squeeze. The company GameStop (GME) was heavily shorted by institutional investors and hedge funds. The total outstanding short was over 100 percent of the float (which means total tradable shares). Over the past few months, GameStop had had a few good news events, and it caused some retail investors to become excited and buy into the company.

Then, an online forum called Wallstreetbets (which at the time had around two million followers) suggested to their audience that they could cause a short squeeze if they all purchased shares of GameStop, and did not sell. The result was amazing. On January 11, 2020, the stock was trading at around $20 per share. On January 27, 2020, the stock hit an intraday day high of $483 per share. In two weeks, the stock had returned over 2,000 percent, and some who traded with options and on margin literally became millionaires in a few weeks.

This scenario was caused by a lot of defrauding. The hedge funds had been artificially deflating the stock price through shorting the stock. The retail investors following Wallstreetbets's recommendation defrauded hedge funds out of $2.5 billion as they covered their short interests at a loss. The trading platforms and marker makers (specifically Citadel) defrauded individual investors by halting trading during peak rush times so as to save their partners from more losses. And as of right now, the whole situation is being investigated by the U.S. Senate Banking Committee to see if anything illegal took place.

Whether they find anyone guilty of crimes or not, the whole situation is a lesson on risk management, gambling, and defrauding your neighbor. I'm certain that in the near future, whole books will be written on this unusual situation. For now, let this be a reminder to you that God's principles, though they may be thousands of years old, are not antiquated. They are still applicable today.

Other Investment Types

There are literally hundreds of types of investments to consider, depending on how creative you wish to be, and how risky you wish to be. Some investments produce significantly higher returns than others, but with those returns come higher risks and higher volatility. Back to the topic of diversification, here are some ways solid investors choose to diversify:

1. Stocks (ownership stakes in public companies)

2. Mutual Funds or Exchange Traded Funds (a collection of multiple stocks)
3. Derivatives (such as options)
4. Commodities (gold, soy beans, etc.)
5. Commodity futures (herds of cattle)
6. Currency arbitrage (Forex markets or cryptocurrencies)
7. Real Estate (property and buildings)
8. Inventory (selling on another's platform such as Amazon)
9. Hard Money lending
10. Angel Investor (first investor in a company that will one day go public)
11. Copyrights, patents, and other royalties
12. Full ownership or partnership of a business
13. Bonds (corporate or municipal debt obligations)
14. Annuities (insurance contracts)
15. CD or High Yield Savings funds (locked up funds for the bank to lend)
16. Co-ops or Reits (smaller investment groups owning shared resources and profits)
17. Mortgage-Backed Securities
18. Cash (held against deflation, or in store for future purchases)
19. Advertisement Platforms (like billboards)

The sky is the limit. And now, you can even invest in companies planning to travel to other planets, so I guess the sky is no longer the limit. The point is, you do not need to feel that one individual asset class is too much risk. You can diversify. At this stage of my life, I have only invested into five of the above-mentioned investment categories. One day, I may have more, or I may decide the five I am in are enough diversification to fit my future goals.

Later, we will discuss the best methods to invest for tax savings.

CHAPTER 5

Surety and Business Partnerships

❦

America is a land of opportunity. One of the greatest opportunities is the ability to start your own business. A business could be something as small as drop-shipping a few items online, to billions of items sold, and billions in revenue. While it is very easy to start a business, it is difficult to prosper in a business.

Investing yourself into a business with your time and money is a risky undertaking. According to the U.S. Bureau of Labor and Statistics (BLS), 20 percent of businesses fail and close their doors in the first two years, 45 percent in the first five years, and 65 percent in the first ten years.[12] This means that if you start a business, you are more likely to fail than to succeed. And the cost of failure is years of your time, as well as large financial loss.

Often, an aspiring entrepreneur is too fearful to pull the trigger and begin a business. The risks are too great. But a partnership may help share the risk and split the load. As of the time of this writing, there are around 30 million small businesses in the

U.S. Of those 30 million, 2 million are classified as a partnership. Whether a business is classified as a partnership or not, the majority of small businesses are partnerships in some form.

There are partnerships all around. A business may "partner" with a bank for financing. They may "partner" with a logistics company for smooth delivery of products. They may partner with a financial institution for payment processing. Individuals also partner with financial advisors to outline a retirement strategy. Employees partner with their employers to create and sell products or services. The most important partnership (outside of a relationship with Jesus Christ) is often a marriage partnership. Partnerships can make or break you financially.

The Bible has a word used for partnership. It's the word "surety." Someone who makes sure (or vouches for) the word of another. In today's application, this is a partnership in which someone is becoming collateral (financially) for the agreements of another, such as when a parent co-signs on student loans for their children (a Parent PLUS loan). Another example might be a parent cosigning on a car loan, or a home loan. In each of these instances, the parent becomes "surety" that the loan will be repaid. If the child defaults, the parent will cover the loss.

Is it right to enter into such a partnership? Is it acceptable to vouch for a loan (become the collateral) for a child to attend college, or to co-sign with a friend to borrow money to start a business?

A Binding Partnership

My son, if thou be surety for thy friend, if thou hast stricken thy hand with a stranger, Thou art snared with the words of thy mouth, thou art taken with the words of thy mouth. (Pr. 6:1-2)

Many parents unwittingly become surety for an unfaithful child. It may not seem at the time that the partnership is really going to affect the partner's life, but it can. When you become surety, or a partner, or a co-borrower, you are trapping (snaring) yourself with the words of your mouth. This verse is trying to convey the serious nature of a partnership.

Several years ago, my friend was renting an apartment with three other people. The four of them were all on the lease. One of the ladies got married, and very suddenly moved out, leaving my friend and the other roommates in a situation where they could not afford the rent. They determined that they needed to break the lease (which comes with some fees). My friend paid her portion of the fees, and of some additional wear and tear fees. A few months later, she received notice that more fees needed to be paid. The other roommates had not paid their portion of the fees, and the bill was due. The other roommates had decided that it was too expensive, and they would just not pay. Eventually they did pay their fees, but this would have affected my friend financially. Even though she had paid her portion, her credit was affected, and possibly legal action could have been taken if the fees were not paid.

When Solomon wrote Proverbs 6, he wanted to remind his son Rehoboam, and us today, that any time you strike hands as "surety," you must be prepared to pay the debt. Any time you sign your name on the line for someone else, be prepared to pay.

A parent may say, "Of course I will sign this loan document as a co-borrower for my son. I love my son." But Solomon had something to say about that too. Love is not a good reason to become surety for another.

> *A friend loveth at all times, and a brother is born for adversity. A man void of understanding striketh hands, and becometh surety in the presence of his friend. (Pr. 17:17-18)*

When to become a Partner

Love is not a good reason to become a financial partner. Indebtedness puts a strain on any relationship. If you owe your parents $100,000 for a business you started, and then you go on an expensive vacation to Disneyland, the investor (your parents) is going to wonder if you are making good on your loan. If you can afford to spend $5,000 on a vacation, why did you not apply that $5,000 toward your debt?

The Bible helps give some guidance on when to form partnerships, and how those partners are to treat one another.

1. Yoked Together

> *Be ye not unequally yoked together with unbelievers: for what fellowship hath righteousness with unrighteousness? And what communion hath light with darkness?*

And what concord hath Christ with Belial? Or what part
hath he that believeth with an infidel? (2 Cor. 6:14)

The word "yoked" refers to the wooden harness joining two animals that are pulling a plow. According to Lancaster Farming,
an individual ox can pull around its own weight on a plow.
But two oxen yoked together can pull around four times their
weight on a plow. The yoke links the animals together, allowing
them to pull more than the sum total of their individual abilities.

Contrariwise, yoking together two incompatible animals will
have a negative impact. Yoking together a mule with an ox will
cause them to pull less than the sum total of their individual
abilities. The mule's height advantage over the ox, and the longer
stride will actually cause the force produced by the mule to be
wasted trying to pull along the ox. The mule will actually hurt
itself working against an ox if they are yoked together on a plow.

Paul uses the symbolism of a yoke to describe partnerships in
the church. In the house of worship, it is vital that all worship-
pers worship the same thing. A Christian cannot join hands
in worship with a Muslim, Buddhist, Mormon, or Animist.
They are not the same. The same is true in a marriage, and the
same is true in a business. Partners in business need the same
focus. As was discussed in Chapter 1, focus will drive your decision making.

If one partner in business is focused on growing the business
through debt or acquisition, and the other partner is content to
remain a small "mom and pop" endeavor, they cannot partner.
If one partner desires cash flow while the other desires book
value, the two cannot partner. If one partner wants to develop

111

a business culture of integrity (Pr. 20:23), and the other is okay with cheating customers, the two cannot partner.

2. Arbitration

Inevitably, there will be conflict in any business partnership. That conflict does not need to be damaging, it can also be a good thing to compare differing opinions for a clearer understanding. But when conflict arises to the point of strife, someone has pride.

> *Only by pride cometh contention: but with the well advised is wisdom. (Pr. 13:10)*

In such instances of contention, or in legal matters, or other improprieties, it may become necessary to involve others to bring a resolution. This can be a very difficult matter financially. If there is perceived financial wrong, our first inclination might be to sue or bring legal charges, but the Bible outlines a process for taking up offenses against a brother.

> *Moreover if thy brother shall trespass against thee, go and tell him his fault between thee and him alone: if he shall hear thee, thou hast gained thy brother. But if he will not hear thee, then take with thee one or two more, that in the mouth of two or three witnesses every word may be established. And if he shall neglect to hear them, tell it unto the church: but if he neglect to hear the church, let him be unto thee as an heathen man and a publican. (Mt. 18:15-17)*

While this passage is specifically for offenses between fellow Christians, it can also be applied to any business partnership.

The first thing to do when there is a problem is to kindly confront the offender. Sometimes, an offender may not even know they have caused an offense. Don't let a small matter (or even a big matter) become an even bigger matter because you never confronted the problem. Make sure that when you take a problem to a partner, you can clearly identify what the problem is, and why you believe it is a problem. If the partnership can come to a resolution, business can continue, and will be stronger. But do not let a problem fester into bitterness.

If the problem in a partnership cannot be resolved between the two parties, then the offended needs to take two or three witnesses and try again. Choose witnesses that have understanding of the matter, or experts in the field. If this does not bring about a resolution, then "bring it to the church." The church is the ruling body for the believers. In a business relationship, you may need to hire an arbitrator. If the offense cannot be resolved with an arbitrator, then the partnership will be dissolved.

It is so important to choose your business partnerships carefully! Choosing an easily offended man, or an angry man, will cause years of strife and heartache, and will cost you money!

3. Taking Offense

The final reason why it is so vitally important to choose good partnerships is that ultimately you may be required to suck it up and take the offense. You may be financially responsible for the mistakes of co-signing on a bad loan. You may be responsible financially for the debts of a failed business. You may be responsible financially for the misdeeds of a former partner. And if you are going to follow the Bible principles, be prepared to let it go.

> *I speak to your shame. Is it so, that there is not a wise*
> *man among you? No, not one that shall be able to judge*
> *between his brother? But brother goeth to law with brother,*
> *and that before the unbelievers. Now therefore there is*
> *utterly a fault among you, because ye go to law one with*
> *another. Why do ye not rather take wrong? Why do ye*
> *not rather suffer yourselves to be defrauded? (1 Cor. 6:5-7)*

All throughout the New Testament we see this principle. It is better to take offense, and be a victim, than it is to take a brother to court and stand up for your rights. When dealing with a business partnership, or a financial loan to a co-borrower, you might have to write off your losses and move on. Better to dissolve a partnership, and save a friendship, or even dissolve the friendship, than to take a brother to court. There may be times when such action is required (such as embezzling), but if it is at all possible, don't take your partner to court.

CHAPTER 6

Work and Rest

⁓

Wealth gotten by vanity shall be diminished: but he that gathereth by labour shall increase. (Pr. 13:11)

The internet is full of advertisements on how to make money quick, and how to retire early. Many such advertisements are nothing more than scams, but some are genuine. However, the question that should really be asked is, "What would God think of this work?"

Work is not a bad word. My generation talks very negatively about their "J-O-B." The Bible, however, speaks very favorably about work. Work was instituted by God before sin came into the world (Gen. 2:15). Work is not bad, in fact, before sin came into the world it was easy and enjoyable. It gave purpose to mankind. It was only after the fall into sin that God said work would be done "in the sweat of thy brow" (Gen. 3:17-19).

Work will be hard if it is done right, but it does not have to be unenjoyable. There are principles in the Bible to help us enjoy our work, and help us bring honor to God while involved in our work.

Ethical Work

Work can be moral, amoral, or immoral. Some occupations (such as a fireman) are moral and upright by their nature. Some others (such as a store clerk) are amoral (neither moral nor immoral). And some jobs are immoral (such as a murder-for-hire hitman).

Several years ago, I had the privilege of showing a man how he could have a relationship with God through Jesus Christ. He gladly received Christ's forgiveness from his sins, and began attending church with me on Sundays. At the time he was unemployed, had a wife, and three small children. After several months in search of work, he secured a job in L.A. as a bouncer for a strip club. He was a baby Christian. I told him he needed to immediately turn down that job and keep looking, but he took the job anyway, with the excuse, "I gotta provide for my family."

Obviously, he immediately quit attending church. Within six months, he and his wife were divorced. In less than a year he had sold (or lost) his home in Lancaster, abandoned his wife and children and was living in L.A. working as a drunken bouncer for a wicked company. I don't know where he is today, because he quit returning my calls and texts years ago. You cannot justify immoral work with the excuse, "I gotta provide for my family."

Many who work in immoral occupations will try to appease their conscience by giving money. I have heard that some drug dealers in Mexico financially support their local Catholic church. They will even go into the Catholic cathedrals to confess their sins, then go right back to their wicked life. You cannot "clean up" your money by giving it to the church. In fact, God specifically forbade the temple from receiving money donated from immoral activities!

> *Thou shalt not bring the hire of a whore, or the price of a dog* [meaning the hire of a male prostitute], *into the house of the LORD thy God for any vow: for even both these are abomination unto the LORD thy God. (Deut. 23:18)*

Back to Chapter 1 on stewardship, God does not need your money! He requires that you serve Him as a good steward of all He gives you. Working in an immoral occupation is squandering the stewardship of life that God had granted to you!

Ethical work extends beyond the job you work, and also applies to the way you work. When you work, do you work well?

> *Servants, be obedient to them that are your masters according to the flesh, with fear and trembling, in singleness of your heart, as unto Christ; Not with eyeservice, as men pleasers; but as the servants of Christ, doing the will of God from the heart; With good will doing service, as to the Lord, and not to men: Knowing that whatsoever good thing any man doeth, the same shall he receive of the Lord, whether he be bond or free. And, ye masters, do the same things unto them, forbearing threatening: knowing that your Master also is in heaven; neither is there respect of persons with him. (Eph. 6:5-9)*

If you are an employee, God requires that you work for your boss as if he were Christ. If you are an employer, God requires that you act toward your employees as if you were Christ. How does this look?

1. Obedience

When you are given a job to do, do it. Unless that job violates a command of God, do it. As an employee, you do not get to decide what job you do. Just because cleaning toilets is not in your job description, does not mean that you can't clean toilets. A good boss will recognize that your best use is probably doing what your job description outlines, but sometimes the more urgent need is a toilet.

I have a very close friend who finished Bible college and believed that God had called him to be a pastor. Upon graduation, he was asked if he would be willing to serve as a janitor for a time while training for ministry in his local church. My friend had to pray about it. He does not want to be a janitor. He wants to serve God as a preacher. But for a season, he has chosen to place himself into a humbling role so that he might learn how to minister to people. He will be a great pastor one day, because he has shown that he can clean toilets.

2. Honor

When Ephesians 5 states "fear and trembling," it does not mean that employees are to be afraid of their boss, but rather that they honor their boss and his wishes. Too many employees gossip or speak badly about their boss. God's Word requires that Christians honor their boss, even if they don't like him or her. And they serve their boss as though they were serving Christ.

This makes an employee ask the question, "What would the boss want?" When I was in college, I worked as a manager in a warehouse for a contracted company that provided "lumper services" for the incoming shipments. My boss worked in the morning hours and was usually gone by the time I arrived for the afternoon shift. It was not easy for me to honor my boss. I believed the only reason he was the boss was because corporate wanted a "yes man" in that position.

Looking back, I realize I was exactly correct in my assumption. Corporate did want a "yes man" in his position. My boss' job was to keep the warehouse management happy with our lumper service, because our contract was worth millions of dollars annually. Other positions dealt with numbers, and production, and efficiency. His job was to appease the warehouse corporate office so that our company could maintain the contract. I did not honor him as I should have. Looking back, I realize that far too often I joked about him with other managers, the whole time missing that he was performing his job exactly as he was intended. He was hired for his position because he was good at appeasing the management of both companies, and smoothing over any tensions that could cost the company its contract.

Honor is not given based upon performance, intelligence, or integrity. Honor is given because you choose to give honor. God commands His children to give honor to their masters (employers) as if they were Christ (Eph. 6:5).

3. Integrity

"Not with eyeservice." This means an employee works hard when the eyes of others are watching, but does not work hard when the eyes are looking elsewhere.

As a manager, I only had one occasion where I ever had to fire someone. A lumper service has a high turnover rate, and several times I recommended to my boss that someone be fired, but only one time did I actually call an employee and tell them they were fired. He was only eighteen years old. In the warehouse, there was a rule that no one could have a cell phone on them except managers.

This new employee knew the rule, because he was told so when he was hired. On his second day at work, I spotted him inside a truck he was supposed to be unloading, checking his phone. I graciously reminded him of the rule, and took the phone to the office and locked it in a drawer so it could not be stolen. On lunch he took the phone out to his car. He understood the rule. I thought he was obeying the rule.

A few days later, after less than two weeks of working for me, I received a call from security. When this new employee thought no one was watching, he was pulling out his phone and texting friends. Security had seen it on the cameras and asked me to remind my employee that phones were not allowed in the warehouse. There was no reminding him the second time. I had been gracious to the new employee the first time; but the second time proved he had no integrity. If he could not be trusted to leave his phone in the locker room or car, then he could not be trusted to work when I was not watching. I fired him.

You may think it was harsh to fire an eighteen-year-old guy for having his phone in a warehouse. No matter how unnecessary the rule may have seemed, his attempts to disguise breaking the rules led me to see him as untrustworthy. If he could not be trusted in such a small matter as a phone, he could not be trusted to work by himself to empty the truck. Integrity matters.

> *The integrity of the upright shall guide them: but the perverseness of transgressors shall destroy them. (Pr. 11:3)*

> *Better is the poor that walketh in his integrity, than he that is perverse in his lips, and is a fool. (Pr. 19:1)*

As an employee or employer, you must labor with integrity. Stealing time is stealing money. Cutting corners may be costing repeat customers. It is not acceptable to cheat someone who may never know they have been cheated because you feel you can get away with it. Integrity is doing right, even when no one sees but God. Integrity will help you transform an amoral occupation into a moral and ethical one.

4. <u>Kindness</u>

Our passage speaks mainly to employers when it states, "forbearing threatening," but it can apply to both employees and employers. Are you a harsh worker? Harsh toward your employees, harsh toward your contractors, harsh toward your customers, harsh toward your family? Everyone will mess up. Do you use others' failures to lord over them, or do you use them to teach and to train others? If you are an employer, eventually, there comes a point where enough grace has been extended, and you may need to terminate employment. But you should always be kind!

Ethical work is not based solely upon the job, a lot is dependent upon the actions and attitudes of the laborer. A thief who steals from a bar would also steal from a church. A gossip who dishonors his boss at the grocery store would also dishonor his boss even working for a church. Are you an ethical worker?

How Much Should I Work?

In 2007, author Tim Ferriss published a book called, *The 4-Hour Workweek*. It was on the New York Times Best Seller List for four years, sold over 2 million copies, and was translated into forty languages. In other words, it was popular. The author is worth over $100 million (according to Forbes), the majority of which came from his business ventures outside of writing. Like many secular books, there are some valuable principles in the book, but I suppose the majority of readers selected the book because of the title. My generation wants to earn a lot, and work a little.

1. Do Not Overwork

Are there biblical principles to how much work ought to be done? Yes. And the principles in the Scriptures may not conform to your desires. All the way back in the beginning, God gave Adam a job to do and told him to do that job six days a week, and rest the seventh day. That command was reiterated to the Jews and placed into their required law as the fourth commandment of the Ten Commandments.

Six days shalt thou labour, and do all thy work: But the seventh day is the Sabbath of the LORD thy God: in it thou shalt not do any work... (Ex. 20:9-10)

God gives a clear command to His people that you must not allow work to interfere with worship! In my life, there was a stretch where I felt like all I did was work, and I was just spinning my wheels, going nowhere. At the time I was a full-time college student, working a full-time job, a part-time job, and pastoring on the weekends. Life was busy. It was also one of the most discouraging times I've had. I did not need to work seventy hours a week. I was working that much because I could. The result was exhaustion and sickness, and I was no better off financially than I had been the previous semester.

What I discovered that January was that God did not design us to work all the time. God designs us to take time to rest and worship. You may be a "workaholic" like I was and still am. You may need to slow down, and take time to rest and worship. I've known many men who chose to work overtime on weekends to get ahead, only to lose their families, their faith, and everything else they cared about. Some seasons will be busier than others, but make sure your priorities are right. Don't develop a spirit of covetousness.

2. <u>Do Not Be Lazy</u>

The majority of people fall into the lazy category (including myself at times). You can be lazy while on the clock (as was mentioned previously about integrity), or you can be lazy and just not want to work. The Bible has a lot to say about those who are lazy.

The sluggard will not plow by reason of the cold; therefore shall he beg in harvest, and have nothing. (Pr. 20:4)

How long wilt thou sleep, O sluggard? When wilt thou arise out of thy sleep? Yet a little sleep, a little slumber, a little folding of the hands to sleep: So shall thy poverty come as one that travelleth, and thy want as an armed man. (Pr. 6:9-11)

Laziness is not defined by hours worked at a job; laziness is defined as "unwilling to work or expel energy."[13] A better explanation might be "unwilling to do what you don't want to do, but need to do." The sluggard who would not plow because it was cold still needed to plow, or he would have no harvest. The sluggard who would not get up from his nap to work will beg like a vagabond in time to come, having nothing to support himself.

Only you can really know how much work is enough to not be lazy, and how much work is too much and keeps you from rest and worship. Work is not defined by the hours on a job, but by what you are busy doing. Is it productive, or not? Is it advancing you toward your God-given purpose, or is it amusement?

Many people work hard for forty to fifty years, all the while saving and investing. They reach an amount they feel can give them a retirement, and they quit their jobs. Once their time is their own, they have no purpose, and thereby waste their golden years doing nothing of any value. Though they might have been called a hard worker, they end by defining themselves as lazy.

3. Retirement in the Bible

There is only one defined "retirement" in the Bible. In Numbers 8:25, God restricted the Levites who served in the tabernacle to be between twenty-five and fifty years old. They were effectively "retired" at age fifty. But their role actually switched from being the laborers to being more like advisors.

And from the age of fifty years they shall cease waiting upon the service thereof, and shall serve no more: But shall minister with their brethren in the tabernacle of the congregation, to keep the charge, and shall do no service. Thus shalt thou do unto the Levites touching their charge. (Num. 8:25-26)

The Levites had no retirement plan, because they were not allowed to purchase land and flocks. They were dependent upon the gifts from the people (tithes) to sustain them during their ministry, and after their ministry ceased. The purpose of their "retirement" was to ensure that strong, capable men were involved in the physically demanding work of sacrificing. They effectively worked until their strength began to wane, and then received "pension" support until their death. But even after their "retirement" they still served the tabernacle, just not the same way as before.

4. Early Retirement

There is a movement among the younger generation to "retire early." What they really mean is that they don't want to work to live life as they want to live. There is also an avalanche of laziness and an epidemic of indecision in the same generation. The three go together hand in hand with a lack of purpose. I have known several friends who went more than a decade to college, but never really figured out what they wanted to do with their life (except retire).

If your purpose is to fund missions work, then work to fund missions work. If your purpose is to travel the world, then work to travel the world. If your purpose is to sit at home watching TV, then you need a new purpose. The lazy want early retirement so they don't have to work. The diligent will take early retirement if they can afford it, to fulfill their God-given purpose. It's okay to aim for early retirement if you have a purpose. If you have no purpose, refer back to Chapter 1 and start over. Until your purpose is settled, retirement is pointless.

Extra Income

Now we come to a favorite topic of mine: "What can I do to earn extra on the side?" I've always been a financial "go getter," but I have not always had the best ideas or goals when it comes to a "side hustle." What does the Bible say in this regard?

> *The soul of the sluggard desireth, and hath nothing: but the soul of the diligent shall be made fat. (Pr. 13:4)*

> *The thoughts of the diligent tend only to plenteousness; but of every one that is hasty only to want. (Pr. 21:5)*

First, are you diligent in your primary employment? If the answer is no, then you do not deserve to work in that employment. Your first job is your first responsibility. If you do not want to work that job, or if that job does not help you achieve the purpose God has set for you, then quit, and find a new job in which you can work diligently. Also, if you are able to perform more at your workplace, then you will likely receive the most return on your work from that job.

I have a friend who is a car salesman (he is one of the good ones). He only sells a few cars every month (that is the nature of the business), but he makes a large commission on each car (especially when that car is a $125,000 Nissan GTR). The first and best use of his time is to figure out how to sell more cars. To go from ten cars in a month to eleven cars in a month will give him a 10 percent boost in his commissions.

Not every employment has the ability to earn more. One summer, I worked as a lumper for a different company than the one during college. At that company, I was paid a percentage of the production I generated. I received 45 percent of the lumper fees for trucks that I unloaded. I made pretty good money ($23 per hour average over the summer of 2008). It was worth it for me to unload and separate as many trucks as possible. I was the first one there in the morning (arriving before 6:00am to receive the first truck), and I was usually the last one there in the afternoon. But the trucks were usually done by 3:00pm. If I wanted to generate more income, I needed a side hustle, because there were no more trucks to offload.

I have done many different "side hustles." Maybe not as many as you have, maybe more. Before discussing side hustles, I want to remind you not to be distracted by the spirit of covetousness. Find your focus, and work toward that goal. The majority of side jobs I have taken have had a purpose. Here are a few things I have done:

1. Collecting Pop Cans to Give for Missions

My parents instilled in me when just a small child the discipline of giving to missionaries. One year when I was in the third grade, I wanted to be a part of sending missionaries around the world to preach the gospel. But what could I do? My parents very wisely helped me to understand that if I was going to promise to help missionaries, then I needed a plan. At the time, Oregon had a $.05 deposit on pop cans, refundable at the store. Many people did not take the time to return their cans because they were only worth a nickel. The plan they gave me was to collect five pop cans each week, turn them in to the bottle return at the store for $.25, and give that to missionaries.

I was not allowed to take pop cans from our house. Those were cans for which my mom had paid the deposit, and she would return them herself. I had to go find five pop cans. So several times a week, my mom or dad would take me and my siblings out for a walk, and I would have a bag for the pop cans I found. When I found five, they took me to the store, I returned the cans for a quarter, and I could give that quarter to the missionary offering every Sunday. It was only a quarter, but to a third-grade boy, it was big time!

2. Reselling Candy Bars for Camp

In the winter months of seventh grade, I was determined to pay my way to Christian camp the upcoming summer. Somehow, I was shown a candy catalog for fundraisers. I determined that I would sell candy bars to go to camp. That spring I sold around 300 candy bars (generating around $.50 profit each) and was able to pay for camp myself. It was at that camp, years later, that God called me to be a preacher.

3. <u>Mowing Lawns for Camp</u>

Once I was in middle school, I was old enough to go to Bible summer camp and to youth conferences, but they were expensive. I remember asking my parents if I could go. They agreed, but I would need to pay my own way. So, I got our lawn mower and went to the neighbor's house. He paid my brother and me $10 each to mow his lawn. I was only eleven years old at the time, and my brother did more work than me, but it was the first time I had earned money mowing a lawn. I then was given opportunities over the next few months to do yard work for other families in our church. I saved the money, and was able to attend Bible youth camp.

4. <u>Car Wash for Missions Trips</u>

My love for mission work continued to grow. When I was just a teenager, in 2002, our youth pastor was taking a trip to Mexico to visit a missionary, and I wanted to go also. There were also two other large youth trips that summer. I wanted to go on all three, but the total cost would be $1,300. That was an insane amount of money for a thirteen-year-old in 2002. Every year our church would host a fundraiser car wash to help the teens raise money for these summer events. Most of the teens would raise enough money for camp (around $150). I wanted to raise all $1,300.

I started going door to door, asking for sponsors. I called everyone I knew, asking for sponsors. And on the day of the car wash I worked as hard as I could so we could hit our goal of 100 cars washed that day. I successfully raised all $1,300 in that one day because I worked hard to find sponsors. None of my other friends even raised $400.

5. Donating Plasma to Help Missionaries

When I completed college, I returned to my home church to serve as an unpaid intern for a year and a half. My expenses were very low (seeing as I was living with my parents in their basement), but I wanted to continue to give to missionaries. A friend of mine told me I could donate plasma, and they would pay me money for my plasma. I had already been donating whole blood, so it was an easy switch to make. That switch allowed me to give when I had no income.

6. Building Houses to Fund Missions Trips

During the time I was an unpaid intern, I met my best friend. He was a builder. He was also interested in travel and took a trip to Ukraine. When he returned, he told me all about his trip, and how he wanted to go help other missionaries around the world. I did too. I had already travelled to several other countries helping missionaries while in college. I wanted to go, but I had no money (I was still an unpaid intern). My friend suggested that I come work for him on my day off, and he would pay for the next trip. After a few months working, we went on a month-long trip to the Philippines and Thailand.

I still periodically work on my days off with this friend to travel to other countries to help missionaries. Since then, I've gone to El Salvador, China, and Brazil, all funded through this side hustle. I have also gained some valuable skills that help me in my other ventures.

7. Flipping Houses to Fund Ministry

Since gaining some construction skills with my best friend, I took the risk of buying a fixer-upper condo. It was not the house my wife and I desired, but it was something we could afford. As a pastor, I need a home where I can be "given to hospitality" (Rom. 12:13; 1 Tim. 3:2). We are on our second house flip, and the proceeds of upgrading fixer-uppers is what will be used to purchase the home we wish to have in the future to fulfill our ministry desires.

8. Collecting Pop Cans to Fund Missions Trips

As a child I collected pop cans to give to missionaries. Now as an adult, I continue to collect pop cans, and return them for the deposit. I average around $200 a year turning in pop cans. It takes around two hours a year to return the cans, and I collect them when I see them. Overall, it is just a little something more to help send me around the world to preach the gospel.

9. Gift Cards for Missionaries

For a time, there were several online gift card retailers that would resell unused gift cards at a discount. Often, I could pur-chase a $100 gift card for $80-$90. I decided I would buy gift cards to places I frequented, but instead of simply using a gift card for my purchases, I would only purchase on the gift card if I had the cash to pay for the items or food. Then, I would "pay back" myself the cash value of the purchase made on the gift card. This would allow me to purchase new gift cards, and to ensure I did not spend money I did not have.

At the end of the year, I purchased several hundred dollars' worth of gas station gift cards with the funds I had saved. I was then able to generously give several hundred dollars' worth of gas to missionaries raising support for foreign work. For no work, I was able to give a substantial offering.

10. Trading Stocks to Fund a Remodel, Missions Giving, and College

I have tried many trading apps, crypto currency exchanges, and other platforms in an attempt to grow investments. These are not funds for my retirement goals, these funds are for short-term projects. This is very risky (see Chapter 2 for more on that story), and requires more time, and more diligence, but so far, the Lord has allowed me to generate profits that have helped to fund my wife's college bill, remodel projects in our fixer-upper, and additional large gifts toward missions projects.

11. Credit Card Points

Most credit card companies have reward programs for using their cards. The credit card company pays out their rewards from their collected merchant fees. They also hope the user will go into debt and pay interest on money borrowed. It is **never** a good idea to carry a credit card balance. However, if you are disciplined with budgeting and tracking your spending, so that you never spend money on a card that you cannot repay from your budget line item, then credit card rewards are a bonus perk.

In the five years my wife and I have been married, we have accumulated close to $5,000 in cash back rewards for spending we would already have done. We pay no interest, we never overspend on the cards, because we only spend what our budget allows, and we receive around $1,000 per year in cash back. This money is applied to our missions travel budget. Rewards points paid for around a quarter of the price of our trip to Brazil to visit missionaries.

12. Other- To Be Announced.

I actually have several other potential moneymaking ventures in the works that have either made no money, or which I am not yet prepared to share. The point is not to give you a list of things you could do, but to help you see that anyone can use their time to generate more wealth if they will have a focus and apply themselves diligently. Just beware the sneaky spirit of covetousness.

Recently, I read a biography on the life of Charles Spurgeon.[14] Included in his biography was a section on the Book-Fund started by his wife, Susanna Spurgeon. Upon reading a particular publication of her husband's, she declared how she wished every pastor in England could have a copy. Mr. Spurgeon responded by asking, "What will you do about it?" Rather than simply making a statement, she was asked to put action to her desire.

She went into her room to a "junk drawer" and pulled out a collection of coins she had been saving with no purpose in particular. It turned out to be a sizable amount of money, enough to purchase 100 copies of the book, and to send them to 100 pastors in England. From that day forward, she made it her life's work to supply books to pastors.

In the drawer, her coins had no value, but put to work, they were the "seed money" to supply thousands of books to pastors around the world, and the catalyst to a new purpose in her life. You never know what God might do through a little creativity, ingenuity, and hard work.

I have friends who have even more unusual methods of earning additional income. Some require hustle and hard work (such as a second job), while others require creativity and discipline (such as credit card churning). There are thousands of ways you could generate extra income to fund your purpose. Those who will be diligent with the stewardship God has entrusted to them will be granted more opportunities to increase that stewardship.

CHAPTER 7

Taxes, Welfare and Government

ℰℐ𝒪

I am not a C.P.A. This is a book outlining the biblical principles of finances. The Bible does speak about taxation, social
welfare, and the role of government. I understand that this book
will not fix the errors of our system, but it may help you to determine how best to approach these topics in your own life.

Purpose of Government

Government is not mentioned in the Bible until after the flood
of Noah. Before the flood, there are two instances where the
roles of government are shown. The first was when God said
that He would protect Cain from the wrath of his family (Gen.
4:15), the second was when Lamach vowed to protect himself
from the wrath of others after he slew a man (Gen. 4:23).

After many generations, the earth was corrupt and wicked. God
saw the wickedness of man, and it grieved Him at his heart
(Gen. 6:5-6). God therefore sent a mighty flood to destroy every
living creature upon the earth, while saving Noah and his family.

After the flood waters subsided, God began to outline the role of government. What is the biblical role of government?

1. Judgment upon the Wicked

> *Whoso sheddeth man's blood, by man shall his blood be shed: for in the image of God made he man. (Gen. 9:6)*

It is very unpopular in our culture today to speak of capital punishment. As of this writing, twenty-five states in the U.S. have a death penalty, twenty-two have no death penalty, and three have governor-imposed moratoriums on the death penalty. You may hold certain opinions about the death penalty, but it was instituted by God as the first duty of government. According to the biblical principles, half of U.S. state governments are failing in their first responsibility.

According to Statista,[15] from 1990-2019 in the U.S. there were 531,348 murder and non-negligent manslaughter cases in the U.S. During that same time there were 1,388 death penalties enforced in the U.S. It is obvious that the U.S. government has neglected the first responsibility of government in favor of other duties.

You might be of the opinion that capital punishment is immoral, but you would be wrong. Morality is defined by God, not man. God has a reason for capital punishment.

> *Because sentence against an evil work is not executed speedily, therefore the heart of the sons of men is fully set in them to do evil. (Ecc. 8:11)*

Capital punishment is designed by God as a corrective mechanism for wicked man. If justice is not measured out quickly, wicked men will wax worse and worse (2 Tim. 3:13). What are the other duties of government outlined in the Bible?

2. Protection of the People

The next few chapters of Genesis give a historical narrative of things occurring, but not any instruction on the purpose of government, until Genesis 14. In Genesis 14, nine little kingdoms go to war. Nothing is said in this passage about who was right or who was wrong. Nothing is said about kept or broken treaties. All that is stated is that five kingdoms served Chedorlaomer, king of Elam, and then rebelled. In response, King Chedorlaomer attacked the five kings who rebelled, and took captives and spoil.

From the narrative, it is assumed that Chedorlaomer attacked out of the pride of his heart, and desire to rule. It appears that it was an unjust war. For that reason, we see Abram got involved. His nephew, Lot, was among those taken captive by King Chedorlaomer. So Abram armed 318 of his servants to pursue, attack, and defeat the armies of Chedorlaomer. (Gen. 14:14-15). Abram then returned the captives to their homes and restored their stolen wealth.

After the victory, God sent His priest, named Melchizedek, to meet Abram, and congratulate him on his victory. It was after meeting with Melchizedek that Abram committed to return all the spoil from the war, save what was spent, and what was given to the Lord. A Bible principle for government was given to us from Genesis 14. Government is intended to protect its people, not enrich its own coffers.

This principle is reiterated during the days of Joseph. God revealed in a vision to Pharaoh the future fourteen years; seven years of plenty, and seven years of famine (Genesis 41). The dream was given as a tool to elevate Joseph into a position of power so that he might save his people from the upcoming famine. During the seven years of plenty, the Egyptian government would tax 20 percent of the food produced in Egypt and store it, so that during the seven years of famine, they might sell it back to the people. The tax was used to protect the people from starvation. (It was also used to secure more control. Whether that was the intention is not clearly defined by the passage.)

3. Example of Worship before God

The third purpose of established government was to give the example of righteous worship before God. This has been such a big failure throughout the years that America was founded specifically as a place of freedom from governmental interference in worship. Were governmental worship to be performed correctly, this could be a great tool for establishing righteousness, but history has proven that it will not be so.

Israel was commanded to worship God and be a light to the heathen world. Instead, they mimicked the heathen, and in many cases even surpassed the wickedness of the heathen! The supposed conversion of Constantine on October 28, 312AD led him to proclaim freedom for Christianity in 313AD. This quickly led to a Church/State marriage, which led to the Roman Catholic Church. Instead of being a beacon of righteousness, the

Catholic Church sought power, compromised doctrine, then abandoned God's Word. She persecuted the true Christians, murdered millions, and spiritually blinded all of Europe for nearly a millennium. Their wickedness is still felt around the world today with a "form of godliness" that follows "another Christ" (2 Tim. 3:5; Mt. 24:4-14).

Government's New Purpose

Most western governments today have completely failed in their first objective to bring judgment upon the wicked. Many are trying to stop the second (protection for its people) by legalizing abortion and euthanasia, and limiting military and defense spending. (I personally believe the government has not been wise with military spending, but it is a part of their God-given responsibility.) And most governments have completely abandoned the third responsibility, because they do not know God. Instead, they have substituted new agendas in place of the old.

1. <u>Keynesian Economics</u>

Money does not stay stationary. As money is passed through hands, it simultaneously makes multiple people wealthy. Not because of the dollar, but because of the time and work used to generate that dollar. If I spend $1,000 purchasing a new phone, that company pays employees for their work, those employees spend their wealth on other goods, and the money circulates. This circulation then becomes more wealth for more people than the original $1,000 could have been.

Keynesian Economics[16] is the idea that governments can create a wealthy and prosperous economy by infusing large stimulus into the system. The government has therefore taken it upon themselves to ensure economic prosperity of its people, a task that was never assigned to them by God.

Many will argue that governmental oversight is essential to a thriving economy, and that can be true. But Keynesian Economics is not the same as governmental oversight. Oversight would be ensuring that companies are ethical. The theory of Keynesian Economics is unethical. How can a government infuse money into their nation's economy? They must either spend that money (thus favoring particular industries) or give away that money (which promotes the welfare mentality discussed later).

2. Infrastructure

All the way back to the tower of Babel, public works projects have been a major focus of governments. However, the first public works project was shut down by God Himself.

> *And the LORD said, Behold, the people is one, and they have all one language; and this they begin to do: and now, nothing will be restrained from them, which they have imagined to do. Go to, let us go down, and there confound their language, that they may not understand one another's speech. So the LORD scattered them abroad from the face of all the earth: and they left off to build the city. (Gen. 11:6-8)*

The purpose of this construction project was to defy God's command to disperse, therefore God would not allow that plan to succeed. This does not mean that God is against all public works, only those that are built in opposition to Him. In 2017, the federal and state governments spent $441 billion on infrastructure projects.[17] That number is mind-bogglingly large, but is actually a small portion of their overall budgets. Many believe that it is not enough.

Is it necessary for governments to spend money on infrastructure? From a biblical standpoint, no. There is no command in the Bible for governments to spend on infrastructure. But neither is there a command not to spend on infrastructure. The real question must be: Who would build the infrastructure (roads, dams, etc.) if not the government?

In the late 1800s and early 1900s, America was ruled by the titans of industry,[18] men like John D. Rockefeller, Cornelius Vanderbilt, Andrew Carnegie, Henry Ford, J.P. Morgan, and others. Infrastructure was built, and therefore controlled, almost exclusively by these men. The result was something that many Americans found undesirable. The greed of big corporations kept the common American worker poor. Not all of these particular men were consumed with covetousness. In fact, some were known for their philanthropy, but the American people wanted the oligarchies broken up. Along came President Theodore Roosevelt, the "Trust Buster," and he did just that.

There is nothing inherently wrong with government infrastructure spending, nor with private industry providing infrastructure. But it was not intended by God to be the primary focus of government.

3. Education

Massachusetts was the first state to pass compulsory school laws in 1852, requiring all children to attend elementary schooling. Prior to 1852, attending school was optional, and many governments did not provide any form of education. In the 1950s, education costs soared as the U.S. Government attempted to educate faster and better than the U.S.S.R. Since then, education costs have only increased.[19] In the 2016-2017 school year, total public school spending amounted to $739 billion, an average of $14,439 per student. College and university costs have also skyrocketed. As of March 2019, total outstanding student loan debt stood at $1.6 trillion in the U.S. It is a governmental priority to educate children, but is it biblical?

The first recorded instance in the Bible of education is the command God gave to Israel in Deuteronomy.

> *And these words, which I command thee this day, shall be in thine heart: And thou shalt teach them diligently unto thy children, and shalt talk of them when thou sittest in thine house, and when thou walkest by the way, and when thou liest down, and when thou risest up. (Deut. 6:6-7)*

The first and primary responsibility for education falls upon the parents, not the government. And the top priority of that education is the Word of God. Sadly, America has eliminated God from the public education system. It has instead infused humanistic philosophies contrary to the Word of God into the curriculum. Public education in America has become so tainted by godless teaching that many Christians feel they cannot send their child to the public school system, because it would be giving their child's mind into the hands of the heathen.

Thus saith the LORD, Learn not the way of the heathen, and be not dismayed at the signs of heaven; for the heathen are dismayed at them. (Jer. 10:2)

Love not the world, neither the things that are in the world. If any man love the world, the love of the Father is not in him. (1 Jn. 2:15)

The first instance in the Bible where a public education system is implemented is found in the book of Daniel:

And the king spake unto Ashpenaz the master of his eunuchs, that the should bring certain of the children of Israel, and of the king's seed, and of the princes; Children in whom was no blemish, but well favoured, and skillful in all wisdom, and cunning in knowledge, and understanding science, and such as had ability in them to stand in the king's palace, and whom they might teach the learning and the tongue of the Chaldeans. (Dan. 1:3-4)

When Nebuchadnezzar instituted this selective education system, it was intended to transform Israelite children into Babylonian leaders. They changed their identity, their language, and their way of thinking to conform to the will of the king. This is no different than the current American education system. Funded by the government, it takes children and conforms them into the image of the world. The American education system is very anti-God, anti-Bible, and anti-biblical principles.

4. Social Welfare

The largest line items in the congressional budget are now social welfare programs. According to the Congressional Budget Office,[20] in 2019 the U.S. federal government spent $4.4 trillion in total. Of that spending, $1 trillion went to Social Security payouts, $1.1 trillion went to Medicare, Medicaid, CHIP, and the ACA marketplace subsidies. Another $361 billion was spent on "safety net programs" such as low-income housing assistance, SNAP (food stamps), school meals, etc. This amounts to more than half the federal budget going to various forms of social welfare.

Social Security is different than other forms of social welfare, because it is a "pay in" system, but the fact remains that it is part of the responsibilities taken upon the government that are not outlined as the primary focus of government as found in the Scriptures. It is not supposed to be the government's job to make sure that the older generation has income. It is the responsibility of the worker to save for the future, and of the children to care for their aging parents.

Back to the biblical mandate God gave to His people, the Jews. "Alms giving" was sufficient for the nation of Israel to completely meet the needs of all social welfare. It was done by commandment, but it was regulated individually. If a Jew saw that a homeless man was a lazy drunkard, that man would not be the recipient of his alms gift. Only those who genuinely needed help would receive it. Those who wished to "game the system" had no system to game. It was work or starve.

*For even when we were with you, this we commanded
you, that if any would not work, neither should he eat. (2
Thess. 3:10)*

Biblical Principles of Taxation

It is often said that there are only two things certain in this
world, death and taxes. Are taxes legal? Is taxation theft? Is it
biblical to pay taxes?

*And Jesus answering said unto them, Render to Caesar
the things that are Caesar's, and to God the things that
are God's. And they marveled at him. (Mk. 12:17)*

When Jesus made this statement, He was living in a country
controlled by a foreign power. His taxes were not going to pay
for the Jewish government, they were going to pay for a wicked
Roman government. The Romans conquered for greed and
power, worshipped devils, and persecuted righteousness. It was
the Roman government who would eventually crucify Jesus on
a Roman cross. And yet Jesus still told those listening to pay
their taxes.

Governments do have the authority to collect taxes based upon
God's Word. But even when it is an illegitimate government, or
one that spends the tax revenue foolishly or wickedly, it is still
biblical that we pay taxes. And what's more, a Christian ought
always to be honest when paying those taxes! It is a matter of
integrity.

In America, and many other countries, we have a freedom that
was unknown to the Jews and early Christians. We have the

benefit of voting for taxation. In my state of Oregon, in the last election, there were eight measures on the ballet to increase taxation in some form. I voted "no" on all eight measures, but seven of those eight passed anyway. I was frustrated, and I still am. I will be paying taxes that I do not want to pay to fund stuff that is wrong and immoral. The taxes are unfair, unjust, unrighteous, and yet I will be paying those taxes. Not because I want to pay them, but because I have to pay them.

If I were the one in charge of the government, if I were the king, the budget would be far smaller, the taxation would be far less, and the government's "job" would be more in line with the biblical requirements. But I am not king of the country, so I will pay my taxes.

Deficit Spending

All major economies of the world follow the same philosophy of economics. The Keynesian philosophy involves deficit spending. Deficit spending is when a government spends more money than it receives. Is deficit spending bad? Is deficit spending biblical?

1. <u>Evolution of Money</u>

Deficit spending is a modern invention. In the Bible times, governments could only spend what they had. Eventually, someone decided to promise money that they did not yet have. It was a tactic used by Alexander the Great to raise an army. He promised his army riches and glory, and he delivered on those promises.

In the Tang dynasty in China (618-907AD),[21] the next step toward our modern financial system was taken: the banknote.

Instead of carrying bulky metal, a merchant could deposit their wealth into a bank and receive a promissory note that the wealth was redeemable. This made a banknote valuable because it was backed by real wealth.

Around 1150AD, the Knights Templar began issuing promissory notes. A pilgrim in Europe could deposit funds into a Templar treasury and receive a document (promissory note) indicating the right to retrieve those funds in the Holy Land. This allowed the pilgrim to travel light, and make his withdrawal of money in another location.

In the 1600s, banks in England began offering bank notes in exchange for storing gold. They then discovered that they could lend out bank notes not backed by gold, because not all the bank notes would be returned simultaneously. This began "Fractional Reserve Banking." A bank may have 50,000 gold coins in their vault, but would offer loans on 100,000 gold coins. In 1695, the English country needed to rebuild their navy after suffering losses to the French. So England established a central bank, and issued debt, promissory notes that they would one day pay back the money they borrowed to fund their war with France.

Fast forward into the 20th Century, and the U.S. (followed by every other major country) decided that their promissory notes did not need to be exchangeable for real gold or silver. The banknotes were good enough. By detaching from real currency, the government gave the central bank the ability to essentially print money.

One more step took place with the digitalization of money. Depositing banknotes into a bank gives me a digital promise that I have bank notes to back the digital currency. All of this has allowed governments (and even people) to spend money that does not exist.

2.   Introduction of Deficit Spending

Deficit spending is debt. We have already examined in depth the biblical stance on debt. Those who owe money are subject to the authority of those who lent the money (Pr. 22:7). The government, however, does not want to be subject to the authority of another. Each government wants to set its own rules. So those in authority have devised a method they believe allows them to spend money they do not have, and owe that money to no one.

The first U.S. record of deficit spending dates back to the Revolutionary War.[22] Our first president, George Washington increased the national debt from $71 million to $82 million. Most presidents have run a national federal deficit. The last president to finish his term having decreased the national deficit was President Calvin Coolidge in 1929. As of October 2020, the U.S. Federal Debt amounted to $27 trillion. This debt is currently at nine times the total collected taxes by the federal government. It is supposed that the government can spend next year's tax revenue today, and "kick the can" down the road to the next guy. So far, they have been right.

Banks have done something similar with "mortgage-backed securities." A bank maintains their balance sheets by calculating debts on one end, and assets on the other. When a bank issues a mortgage, it basically creates money. It creates a debt on one side of their ledger and an asset on the other to balance the books. It is digital money that never actually existed. The bank can then package those debts into mortgage-backed securities, and sell them to investors. They have digitally "created money."

Conclusions Drawn

Modern government does not act in accordance with God's laws, and yet we still are required to pay taxes. You cannot control how others may act, but you can choose to abide by biblical principles. Even though others may live a life of covetousness, you must not. Even though others may live a life of accruing debts, you must not. Even though others abandon God's Word you must not. God's Word is the best plan. One day, nations will see their fiscal "house of cards" come crashing down. Will they then seek the wisdom from on High?

CHAPTER 8

Tax Strategies

⌒⌒

Building wealth God's way requires a godly focus (your purpose), a generous spirit (not a spirit of covetousness), long-term thinking, good partnerships, and ethical work. If you follow all of these principles laid out in Scripture, God will provide for you, and give you (financially) all that you need.

I have been young, and now am old; yet have I not seen the righteous forsaken, nor his seed begging bread. (Ps. 37:25)

But there are also other strategies that need to be considered if you wish to achieve maximum success in your godly endeavors. One of the most important financial considerations is taxes. We have already determined that you will pay taxes, but there are legal and ethical ways to limit your tax liability.

I am not a tax professional. I do not have all wisdom, especially when it comes to the tax code. But here are a few basic tax considerations when determining how to build and invest wealth.

Consider Roth vs Traditional Investment vehicles

The "Title 26" document (containing current U.S. Tax Code) currently sits at 6,550 pages in length. Tax law is complex and confusing. This document lists all the tax brackets, tax exemptions, and tax credits applicable to individuals, and each type of business. Out of all those pages, there are a few sections that are particularly important in regard to growing long-term wealth and tax savings.

For centuries, and even millennia, a common source of reoccurring income was a pension. Pension plans date back into the Dark Ages, specifically given most commonly to soldiers in service to a country or the Papacy, to church leaders out of the Roman Church coffers, or paid out to children from a family estate (an allowance). In the modern era, pensions were often guaranteed to employees from their large employer companies.

In 1961, public education employees were granted a special provision in the Internal Revenue Code section 403(b), which allowed them to deposit part of their salaried compensation into an annuity (more on annuities later), which would pay out in retirement. This was a tax advantaged retirement plan, because employees would not pay taxes on their contributions into the 403(b) annuity. Upon retirement, they would pay taxes upon the received benefits from their annuity plan.

In 1974, the United States passed the Employee Retirement Income Security Act (ERISA). The ERISA made provisions to the 403(b) allowing contributions to be invested into mutual funds, in addition to annuities. The ERISA also established the Individual Retirement Account (IRA). The IRA allowed workers in any job to deposit part of their compensation into an investment account, and claim a deduction on their annual tax liability. Essentially, money in the IRA was not yet "earned" in the eyes of the government, and was thereby not yet subject to taxation. The investments could then grow (or diminish) tax-deferred. Then later (upon retirement), the investment could be withdrawn, and taxes would be paid as though it was earned income.

In 1978, the Revenue Act unintentionally created the 401(k). The Internal Revenue Code section 401(k) allowed employees to request that their employers send part of their compensation directly to an investment account before paying any taxes. The 401(k) plan worked the same as the IRA, allowing investments to grow tax-deferred. Taxes would then be paid at the time of withdrawal. The major benefit to a 401(k) plan was that employees would not receive the wages and be forced to contribute into the IRA themselves. Instead, their contributions would be sent to the 401(k) directly. This helped those less disciplined to contribute toward retirement without the temptation of spending the money in hand.

The federal government wanted to encourage employee contributions into 401(k) plans, so in 1981, they added additional tax benefits to the employers who offered these plans. This made them skyrocket in popularity. They also became a popular part of employer compensation packages by including "employer match" to contributions made. By way of example, an employer may guarantee to an employee that they will contribute additional money into a 401(k) plan if the employee contributes.

These plans, the 403(b), IRA and 401(k) all were "tax-deferred" accounts. In 1997, Senator William V. Roth Jr. introduced Public Law 105-34, which established the Taxpayer Relief Act. This allowed employees to choose if they would pay taxes on their investments upon retirement or before retirement. The benefit to paying before retirement would be that all gains in the investment account would be tax-free, having already paid tax on the original contributions. This established the ROTH IRA, ROTH 401(k), ROTH 403(b). There are also other retirement vehicles such as the SEP IRA and 457 plan, which are much less common.

An IRA and a 401(k) work essentially the same way. When choosing what type of a retirement account you wish to set up, the bigger consideration is whether you will have a ROTH account, or a traditional (non-ROTH) account. Do you want to pay taxes now, or later?

1. Benefits of a Traditional Account

There are two main benefits to a traditional, tax-deferred retirement account. The first is that the contributions made (at time of deposit) are higher than the contributions made into a ROTH account. If an employee is in a 22 percent federal and 9 percent state tax bracket (as I happen to be), then contributions into a traditional retirement account will be 31 percent higher than into a ROTH account. $1,000 earned through employment can equal $1,000 contributed into a traditional account. In a ROTH account, the same $1,000 earned will be taxed first, leaving only $690 to be contributed into the ROTH account. If I wish to contribute $1,000 into a ROTH account, I will need to earn $1,450 dollars at my employment, pay the 31 percent in taxes, and then invest the remaining $1,000. For this reason, it is easier to contribute more money into a traditional investment account than into a ROTH account. The larger initial contribution will (in theory) produce a larger total return value.

The second advantage of a traditional retirement account is that the deposited funds save taxation in the highest tax bracket, to be later spent in a (supposedly) lower tax bracket. For example, the 2020 federal income tax bracket on earning between $85,526 and $163,300 is 24 percent. Every dollar earned beyond that $163,300 will be taxed (federally) as 32 percent. That is an 8 percent increase. If an employee earns $180,000 of taxable income, the last $16,700 will be taxed in the high 32 percent bracket. If instead, the employee contributes $16,700 into a tax-deferred traditional 401(k) plan, he would pay no taxes upon deposit for the contribution amount. Then in retirement, the retiree will withdraw those funds (and growth) entirely in the lower tax bracket (assuming the federal tax bracket percentages do not change). The retiree thereby secures an 8 percent tax savings, having only to pay 24 percent in retirement rather than 32 percent on the earned income at time of deposit.

There is, however, a downside to this strategy. The supposed tax savings will only be realized if the tax brackets actually work in their favor. If taxable liabilities increase, or if the government changes the tax brackets, then it is conceivable that no tax savings will be realized, or that a tax loss will incur. It is a risk, but especially for high income earners, it is a calculated risk with an expected benefit.

2. Benefits of a ROTH Account

A ROTH account (whether IRA or 401(k)) applies contributions after taxes have been paid. The benefit is that all funds in the account are considered to have already been taxed. Therefore, if the account grows substantially large, the funds withdrawn will not be subject to taxation, even though they may be in a higher tax bracket. A ROTH account is especially beneficial to those who are in a low tax bracket, but expect to be in a higher tax bracket in the future.

My wife and I contribute into a ROTH account, because we are in a low tax bracket. I expect that one day, if the Lord allows my investments to grow substantially, those funds would be subject to higher taxation than I currently pay. For this reason, I choose to contribute to ROTH accounts for retirement.

3. Contribution Limits

The U.S. Government wants their taxes. So they have set limits upon the amount a worker can contribute into various retirement accounts. The government also has limits on contributions based upon employee income. The limits are surprisingly low. As a single twenty-four-year-old guy, I maxed out my ROTH IRA contribution limits. Due to my stage of life, I have not always maxed out my contributions, but it is possible, even with a low income.

A 401(k) plan has higher contribution limits. It is very unusual for someone to max out their 401(k) contributions unless they are a high-income earner. In 2020, the ROTH IRA contribution limit was $6,000 (if under fifty years old), and the 401(k) limit was $19,500. A 403(b) plan is also limited to $19,500, and a SEP IRA is limited to $57,000. Talk to a professional investment advisor if you would like more details on these topics.

4. Distributions from Retirement Accounts

It is usually best to wait until retirement to withdraw funds from a retirement account. If funds are withdrawn early, they usually incur a penalty, as well as some additional taxation. There are ways to "borrow" from a 401(k) and other retirement plans, but that is usually not the best financial decision either. A ROTH IRA has a provision that allows the contributor to withdraw any contributed funds without penalty or fines, but all growth must remain in the account until retirement age.

There are a few exceptions to these rules. A first-time home purchase, college expenses, and birth or adoption expenses are occasions where these funds can be withdrawn without penalty from a ROTH account. For a 401(k) account, there are a few instances where withdrawal is also allowed without incurring a penalty.

In general, retirement funds should not be withdrawn until retirement age, however, I have personally broken this rule. In 2016, my new wife and I were looking to purchase our first home (which was also an investment in a fixer-upper). Our limited income made it very difficult to find anything we knew we could afford, and we had virtually no down payment. We chose to take advantage of the ROTH IRA exception to withdraw funds for a down payment. I regret today that we had to pull those funds, but it was a very good decision. The increase in value we received from our first home when we sold, as well as a place to live, meant that our withdrawal was a good decision. Even though those funds never had a chance to increase in the market, they did increase in the value of our home.

Annuities, HSAs and Insurance

Insurance plans are one of the most confusing, and sometimes expensive, parts of investing. Many insurance plans are packaged and presented as if they are investments, when they are not. This will **not** be a comprehensive guide through the insurance world, just a tiptoe into the murky waters. First, we need to ask the question: "Should a Christian have insurance?"

For we walk by faith, not by sight: (2 Cor. 5:7)

A prudent man forseeth the evil, and hideth himself: but the simple pass on, and are punished. (Pr. 22:3)

As a Bible-believing Christian, I live my life by faith. I trust God entirely by faith to meet my needs both today, and in the future. But the Bible is also very clear that preparation is necessary for the future. Those who do not prepare for the future are the "simple ones" who are punished. I believe there is a time for Christians to live by faith, but there is also a time for Christians to prepare for the worst.

It was common in the 1800s and even early 1900s for white western missionaries to die trying to reach the lost souls of Africa, Asia, and the Caribbean countries. Sometimes they died as martyrs at the hands of natives, but more often they died from diseases they were not accustomed to; chiefly malaria. It was common for missionaries, when leaving for the mission field, to pack all their belongings in coffins. They fully expected to be buried in their coffins in the near future.

Walter Gowan of the Sudan Interior Mission wrote in his diary on August 9, 1894:

> *"Written in view of my approaching end, which has often lately seemed so near but just now seems so imminent & I want to write while I have the power to do it. Well Glory to God! He has enabled me to make a hard fight for the Soudan and although it may seem like a total failure and defeat it is not! We shall have the victory & that right speedily. I have no regret for undertaking this venture and in this manner my life has not been thrown away. My only regrets are for my poor dear mother..."*[23]

The person who is wise will plan for the future, even if that future is death. So there is a place for insurance. All drivers in the U.S. are required to carry liability insurance for their driving. All homeowners who possess a mortgage are required to carry home owners insurance. Some businesses are required to provide their employees with health insurance. But what about the various insurances that are not required?

1. Life Insurance

The most common "non-required" form of insurance is life insurance. According to LIMRA,[24] 59 percent of American adults have some life insurance. Not all insurance is the same, and not all insurance is even necessary. The purpose of life insurance is to provide the needed financial support for one's spouse or offspring in the event the insurer perishes before having provided sufficient financial support of their own ability. If I were to die today, I want to ensure that I have provided for my wife so that she is not destitute.

In the Bible, there was only one form of life insurance, it was the continual care by the church!

If any man or woman that believeth have widows, let them relieve them, and let not the church be charged; that it may relieve them that are widows indeed. (1 Tim. 5:16)

When a man died before having accumulated sufficient wealth to support his wife, or if his children were unwilling to take on the task, it fell to the church to care for the widows. It was not the responsibility of the church to care for all widows, but only for the widows who had no other means or support. This act of caring for widows fell first upon the children, and then upon the church when necessary.

In regards to life insurance, there is only one reason someone might need life insurance. If you do not have enough money to provide for your spouse or children in the event that you were to die. Life insurance is for young people, not old people. When I was a twenty-two-year-old single man, I did not have any life insurance. Not because I had no risk of death (I probably had more risk then, than I do now), but because I had no one for whom I needed to provide. I got life insurance the month I got married, because I moved from being totally independent to having someone dependent upon me.

After we were married, we had no life insurance on my wife. Not because she had no risk of death, but because she had no one financially dependent upon her. I could financially provide for myself if my wife suddenly passed away. But recently, we purchased life insurance upon my wife in preparation for the day when we will have children. Until we have sufficient wealth to care for our eventual children after our passing, it is necessary that we have life insurance to provide for our children in case we die prematurely. We would not want to place a financial burden upon their future guardians were we to pass away.

Not everyone needs life insurance. If you have a wealth nest egg large enough to care for all those dependent upon you after your passing, you do not need life insurance. I have a friend who is still in his twenties and does not have life insurance. He is on his way to very quickly becoming a millionaire through his business. Were he to pass away today, his wife would be financially set for at least ten years. But his wife would likely live for another sixty years. It is therefore important that he get life insurance until he reaches a place where his assets can support his wife after his passing. At that point, he will no longer need life insurance.

There are various types of life insurance. There is "term life insurance" and there is "whole life insurance." Term life insurance is the insurance everyone needs if they do not have enough wealth to support their spouse or dependents were they to pass away. The cost is set annually for the duration of the policy with a set benefit. For instance, my policy is a thirty-year term policy (expires in 2050) with an annual premium of about $300. I will pay $9,000 over the next thirty years for this policy (if I live that long), and I will receive no benefit at all if I live beyond that time. The goal is to never use that policy!

Whole life insurance is a little more complicated. Whole life insurance is a life insurance policy with an investment component. It essentially requires a premium that is invested on behalf of the recipient. The policy then has a "cash value" component. It seems like this could be a good investment strategy, but it really is not. As of the time of this writing, there are no companies offering whole life policies that are better than other retirement accounts. Usually, the returns are significantly lower than retirement accounts due to the high fees, and they have no tax advantage unless you are super wealthy, and thereby do not need a life insurance policy.

2. HSA (Health Savings Account)

A health savings account (HSA) is a tax-advantaged account for healthcare needs. If you have the ability to invest in an HSA, then do it. The government allows all money contributed into an HSA to be tax-deductible upon contribution, and spent tax-free upon distribution so long as the distributions are to cover medical expenses.

If you live a long life, you are most likely going to accrue medical expenses. An HSA can therefore be used like a medical retirement account, if the funds are not needed in the short term for medical expenses. It is always a good idea to have an HSA.

3. Annuities

An annuity is an insurance vehicle. Essentially, it combines investments with insurance. Money is placed into the annuity as if it were an investment. The issuer then guarantees a certain return. The annuity becomes "risk-free" monthly income for retirement. In recent years, many annuities have become much more complex in their terms and usage. For instance, an annuity may choose to guarantee a 4 percent return, but also offer up to an 8 percent return in the event that the investment value increased. This annuity would thereby have a "risk-free" 4 percent component with a "stock market weighted risk" of 4 percent.

Annuities can be a good investment strategy for risk-averse investors. There are a few things to consider before purchasing an annuity. First, does the annuity have a rider benefit? Many annuities are attached only to the purchaser and spouse. Upon the death of the purchaser and spouse, there will be no benefit passed on to the heirs. This leaves no risk for you, but it could be a low return investment if you pass away too soon after purchasing the annuity. And in fact, that is what the company is hoping will occur.

Other considerations for annuities include associated fees, living benefits (such as long-term care), legacy benefits, and hundreds of rider options. In the 2020 market, annuities are not suitable investments for many investors. Consult with a fiduciary consultant before purchasing such vehicles.

Tax Strategies

After speaking on so many different topics, is there a best and biblical practice for tax shelters, insurance, and retirement investing? The answer is yes. The individual plan will differ for each family dependent upon their individual circumstances, but here are a few biblical and practical considerations:

1. <u>Pay What You Owe, but Nothing More Unless You Choose</u>

The benefit of the U.S. Government tax laws are that they are public. You have the ability to search out and find every tax dollar you owe, and you have the right to claim certain deductions. The government allows it! Do not defraud the government of what is owed them, even if you think they do not deserve it! Rome certainly did not deserve taxes from the King of Kings and Lord of Lords, yet Jesus paid taxes anyway. Take the opportunity to include any allowances that the government provides and write off as many deductions as you are legally permitted. Hire a tax professional if needed.

2. <u>Identify If You Would Rather Pay Taxes Before Investing or After</u>

Don't assume that the 401(k) is the best option, and don't assume that the ROTH IRA is the best option. Do the math. Count the cost. It is not just money on the line, you need to take into account your purpose and goals. A wrong decision today could be a million-dollar mistake in the future.

3. <u>Paying Taxes Is Good</u>

I don't mean that you want to pay taxes, but the requirement to pay taxes is an indication that you earned money. It is better to be the payer of taxes than the receiver of taxpayer benefits. Non-productive people don't pay taxes, but they receive unequitable tax benefits.

As a children's pastor, I go into run-down, state-sponsored apartment complexes to visit children who ride a bus to church.

Sometimes I look at the fancy cars driven by people on welfare and think, "I would like to drive a car like that." Sometimes I see the food they eat and think, "They eat better than I do. Why don't I get food stamps?" But then I remember, I will not exchange my integrity for the goods of this world. It is a good thing that I pay and not receive, for it means God has blessed me in such a way that I do not need the handout.

Conclusion

⁄⁄

T he Bible is an ancient book, but it is not a dead book. The everlasting, ever-loving, and ever-living God of the Bible has given a living book to guide us in the way we ought to go. The principles contained in the Scriptures are every bit as applicable today as when they were given to mankind. They do not agree with the philosophies of this world, because the world's financial systems are guided by covetousness. The "god of this world" has his fingers intrinsically intertwined with the monetary system of this world.

Every Christian ought to strive to live out biblical principles in all areas of life. Having purpose and understanding your stewardship responsibilities will give you clarity, peace and contentment in your financial life.

If you have not been faithful in the stewardship God has given to you, it is not too late to start! Find your purpose for the assets God has given to you. Make out your budget according to His purposes. Plan for the future, including God in those plans. And especially learn to follow God's leading.

As is often said: "A failure to plan is a plan to fail." If you do not tell your money what to do, it will disappear. I leave you with this thought from Haggai 1:5-6

> *Ye have sown much, and bring in little; ye eat, but ye have not enough; ye drink, but ye are not filled with drink; ye clothe you, but there is none warm; and he that earneth wages earneth wages to put into a bag with holes. Thus saith the LORD of hosts; Consider your ways. (Hag. 1:5-6)*

Bibliography

⚜

(2020, December 20). Retrieved from Congressional Budget Office: https://www.cbo.gov/topics/budget

Alcorn, R. (1989). *Money, Possessions and Eternity.* Carol Streams, IL: Tyndale House Publishers.

Alcorn, R. (2001). *The Treasure Principle.* Multnomah Publishers. Sister, OR

Amadeo, K. (2020, November 5). *US Debt by President by Dollar and Percentage.* Retrieved from The Balance: https://www.thebalance.com/us-debt-by-president-by-dollar-and-percent-3306296

Bainton, R. H. (1955). *Here I Stand A Life of Martin Luther.* New York: Abingdon Press.

Barnier, B. (2020, April 30). *Keynesian Economics.* Retrieved from Investopedia: https://www.investopedia.com/terms/k/keynesianeconomics.asp

Burkett, L. (1975). *Your Finances in Changing Times.* Campus Crusade for Christ.

Charles Spurgeon. (n.d.).

Committee, H. B. (2019, October 22). *Strong Infrastructure and a Healthy Economy Require Federal Investment.*

Retrieved from House Committee on the Budget: https://budget.house.gov/publications/report/strong-infrastructure-and-healthy-economy-require-federal-investment

Department, S. R. (2021, February 24). *Number of Executions in the United States*. Retrieved from Statista: https://www.statista.com/statistics/271100/number-of-executions-in-the-us

Dictionary, O. (2020). *Oxford Dictionary*. Oxford: Lexico.

DQYDJ. (2020, December 16). *Historical Home Prices: Monthly Median Value in the US from 1953-2020*. Retrieved from DQYDJ: https://dqydj.com/historical-home-prices/

Editors, H. (2020). Jamestown Colony. *History.com*.

Franklin, B. (1986). *The Way to Wealth*. Bedford: Applewood Books.

Giovanetti, E. (2019, December 27). *Americans Racked Up $1325 in Holiday Debt in 2019*. Retrieved from magnifymoney.com: https://www.magnifymoney.com/blog/news/2019-holiday-debt-survey

Gross Domestic Philanthropy. (2016, January). *Charities Aid Foundation*, p. 7.

History.com. (2020, December 20). *8 Things You May Not Know About Money*. Retrieved from History.com: https://www.history.com/news/8-things-you-may-not-know-about-money

IQ, C. (2019). *The Bolthouse Foundation*. Bakersfield, CA: The Bolthouse Foundation.

Jr., J. F. (1978). *Giving God's Way*. Wheaton, IL: Tyndale House Publishers.

Kagan, J. (2020). Four Percent Rule. *Investopedia*.

Kirchheimer, S. (2008, June 6). *Payday Lenders Target Social Security Recipients*. Retrieved from aarp.org: https://www.aarp.org/money/scams-fraud/info-06-2008/scam_alert_payday.html

Klampe, M. (2016, April 27). Working longer may lead to a longer life, new OSU research shows. *Oregon State University Newsroom*.

LIMRA. (2020, June 2). *2020 Insurance Barometer Study Reveals a Significant Decline in Life Insurance Ownership Over the Past Decade*. Retrieved from LIMRA: https://www.limra.com/en/newsroom/news-releases/2020/2020-insurance-barometer-study-reveals-a-significant-decline-in-life-insurance-ownership-over-the-past-decade/

MacGregor, J. (2019). *Business Biographies and Memories Titans of Industry.* Sheridan, WY: Cac Publishing LLC.

Martin, J. (2008). *Giving Wisely*. Last Chapter Publishing. Sister, OR

McIntyre, G. (2020, November 20). *What Percentage of Small Businesses Fail?* Retrieved from Fundera: https://www.fundera.com/blog/what-percentage-of-small-businesses-fail

Miles, L. (2013, April 10). *Pack Your Coffins... Let's Go*. Retrieved from Miles In Missions: https://milesinmissions.wordpress.com/tag/walter-gowans/

Rainer, T. S. (2019, June 19). *Just How Bad Is the Summer Slump?* Retrieved from Church Answers: https://churchanswers.com/blog/just-how-bad-is-the-summer-slump-six-discoveries

Ramsey, D. (2003). *The Total Money Makeover*. Nashville, TN: Thomas Nelson Inc.

Robbins, M. (1982). *A Man and His Money*. Schaumburg, IL: Regular Baptist Press.

Sisk, D. (1981). *Right Thinking About Money*. Chattanooga, TN: BIMI Publications International.

Speer, M. L. (1975). *A Complete Guide to the Christian's Budget*. Nashville, TN: Boardman Press.

Writters, S. (2020, August 11). *Understanding the Rising Costs of Higher Education*. Retrieved from Best Value Schools: https://www.bestvalueschools.com/understanding-the-rising-costs-of-higher-

Endnotes

1   Bainton, R. H. (1955). *Here I Stand A Life of Martin Luther.* New York: Abingdon Press.

2   Klampe, M. (2016, April 27). Working longer may lead to a longer life, new OSU research shows. *Oregon State University Newsroom.*

3   Giovanetti, F. (2019, December 27). *Americans Racked Up $1325 in Holiday Debt in 2019.* Retrieved from magnifymoney.com: https://www.magnifymoney.com/blog/news/2019-holiday-debt-survey

4   Rainer, T. S. (2019, June 19). *Just How Bad Is the Summer Slump?* Retrieved from Church Answers: https://churchanswers.com/blog/just-how-bad-is-the-summer-slump-six-discoveries

5   Gross Domestic Philanthropy. (2016, January). *Charities Aid Foundation*, p. 7.

6   Kirchheimer, S. (2008, June 6). *Payday Lenders Target Social Security Recipients.* Retrieved from aarp.org: https://www.aarp.org/money/scams-fraud/info-06-2008/scam_alert__payday.html

7   Editors, H. (2020). Jamestown Colony. *History.com.*

8   Kagan, J. (2020). Four Percent Rule. *Investopedia.*

9   IQ, C. (2019). *The Bolthouse Foundation*. Bakersfield, CA: The Bolthouse Foundation.

10 MacGregor, J. (2019). *Buisness Biographies and Memoris Titans of Industry*. Sheridan, WY: Cac Publishing LLC.

11 DQYDJ. (2020, December 16). *Historical Home Prices: Monthly Median Value in the US from 1953-2020*. Retrieved from DQYDJ: https://dqydj.com/historical-home-prices/

12 McIntyre, G. (2020, November 20). *What Percentage of Small Businesses Fail?* Retrieved from Fundera: https://www.fundera.com/blog/what-percentage-of-small-businesses-fail

13 Dictionary, O. (2020). *Oxford Dictionary*. Oxford: Lexico.

14 *Charles Spurgeon*. (n.d.).

15 Department, S. R. (2021, February 24). *Number of Executions in the Unisted States*. Retrieved from Statista: https://www.statista.com/statistics/271100/number-of-executions-in-the-us

16 Barnier, B. (2020, April 30). *Keynesian Economics*. Retrieved from Investopedia: https://www.investopedia.com/terms/k/keynesianeconomics.asp

17 Committee, H. B. (2019, October 22). *Strong Infrastructure and a Healthy Economy Require Federal Investment*. Retrieved from House Committee on the Budget: https://budget.house.gov/publications/report/strong-infrastructure-and-healthy-economy-require-federal-investment

18 MacGregor.

19 Writters, S. (2020, August 11). *Understanding the Rising Costs of Higher Education*. Retrieved from Best

Value Schools: https://www.bestvalueschools.com/ understanding-the-rising-costs-of-higher-education

20 (2020, December 20). Retrieved from Congressional Budget Office: https://www.cbo.gov/topics/budget

21 History.com. (2020, December 20). *8 Things You May Not Know About Money*. Retrieved from History.com: https://www.history.com/news/8-things-you-may-not-know-about-money

22 Amadeo, K. (2020, November 5). *US Debt by President by Dollar and Percentage*. Retrieved from The Balance: https://www.thebalance.com/ us-debt-by-president-by-dollar-and-percent-3306296

23 Miles, L. (2013, April 10). *Pack Your Coffins... Let's Go*. Retrieved from Miles In Missions: https://milesinmissions. wordpress.com/tag/walter-gowans/

24 LIMRA. (2020, June 2). *2020 Insurance Barometer Study Reveals a Significant Decline in Life Insurance Ownership Over the Past Decade*. Retrieved from LIMRA: https://www. limra.com/en/newsroom/news-releases/2020/2020-insurance-barometer-study-reveals-a-significant-decline-in-life-insurance-ownership-over-the-past-decade/

CPSIA information can be obtained
at www.ICGtesting.com
Printed in the USA
FSHW010638170921

9 781662 826870